Penguin Books
A Rose for Winter

Laurie Lee was born in Gloucestershire and educated at
Slad village school and at Stroud central school. He has
published three books of poems: *The Sun My Monument*
(1944), *The Bloom of Candles* (1947), and *My Many-Coated
Man* (1955). His other works include *Land at War*, written
for H.M.S.O. in 1945, *The Voyage of Magellan*, *A Rose
for Winter*, *The Firstborn*, and *As I Walked Out One
Midsummer Morning*. His *Cider with Rosie*, which has
sold nearly a million copies, is a recommended text for
English study in schools. Fond of travelling and music,
Laurie Lee divides his time between Slad and Chelsea, and
writes from ten in the morning until half past four in
the afternoon without a break.

'Out of a winter in Southern Spain, Mr Lee has spun a magnificent book, outstanding even in a field where the competition is oppressively brilliant' – *New Statesman*

'Mr Laurie Lee has the poet's assurance and originality in the use of words. He also has the artist's eye. His writing, prose or poetry glows and flames with colour. ... This is a book warmly recommended to all who enjoy strong and lively writing with the warmth, colour, drama and humour of the South' – *C. V. Wedgewood*

'A delightful little book. . . It communicates that sharp electric thrill which comes only from Spain' – *Maurice Richardson*

Laurie Lee

A Rose for Winter

Travels in Andalusia

Penguin Books

Penguin Books Ltd, Harmondsworth,
Middlesex, England
Penguin Books Australia Ltd, Ringwood,
Victoria, Australia

First published by Hogarth Press 1955
Published in Penguin Books 1971
Copyright © Laurie Lee, 1955

Made and printed in Great Britain by
C. Nicholls & Company Ltd
Set in Linotype Pilgrim

This book is sold subject to the condition that
it shall not, by way of trade or otherwise, be lent
re-sold, hired out, or otherwise circulated without
the publisher's prior consent in any form of
binding or cover other than that in which it is
published and without a similar condition
including this condition being imposed on the
subsequent purchaser

To Cathy and the Benefactor

Acknowledgements are due to the B.B.C. and the London Magazine for permission to use certain material in this book.

Contents

1. Los Especiales - Algeciras

A brilliant November morning with a sky of diamond blue above the bay and the red flowers of a long summer still glowing darkly on the Rock. The intense blackness of the lampless night had rolled away to reveal, incandescent on the northern horizon, the country we had come to seek. It crouched before us in a great ring of lion-coloured mountains, raw, sleeping and savage. There were the scarred and crumpled valleys, the sharp peaks wreathed in their dusty fires, and below them the white towns piled high on their little hills and the empty roads running crimson along the faces of the cliffs. Already, across the water, one heard, or fancied one heard, the sobbing of asses, the cries and salty voices cutting through the thin gold air. And from a steep hillside rose a column of smoke, cool as marble, pungent as pine, which hung like a signal over the landscape, obscure, imperative and motionless.

So we left Gibraltar to its trim English streets, to its Genoese money-changers, Maltese tobacconists, Hindu silk-merchants and crook-boned Cockney soldiers, and we went down to the quay and gathered our bags and boarded the ferry for Spain.

The ferry flew the Spanish flag, had paddle-wheels, and was old, black-funnelled and squat as a duck. It was the type one might have seen, a hundred years ago, running missionaries up the Congo, loaded with whips and bibles. But today, being Saturday, it was packed to the rails with smugglers. As we moved across the oil-blue waters, innocent in the naked sun, they disposed their Gibraltar loot about them. Strapped to their limbs, under their clothes, went cigarettes, soap, sweets, tinned milk, coffee, corned beef and jars of jam. Then the port of Algeciras drew near, and fishermen cried to us from their boats, and we bounced off a yacht, bumped heavily against the quay, and tied up in a tangle, and landed.

The acid-yellow stones, the quay littered with straw and palms, the green-cloaked policemen carrying pistols, the lax and amiable formalities of passports and customs; then we stood free at last upon the ground, surrounded by Spain and the smell of fish-boxes. I turned then and spoke, after many years, my first words of Spanish, to a porter, and we understood each other. We bargained, our baggage was loaded on to a hand-cart, and we entered the town.

And here was the scene so long remembered: the bright façades still crumbling in the sun; the beggars crowding the quaysides, picking up heads of fish; the vivid shapely girls with hair shining like pitch; the tiny, delicate-stepping donkeys; and the barefoot children scrambling around our legs. Here were the black signs charcoaled starkly on the walls: 'Pension La Africana'; 'Vinos y Comestibles', 'España Libre', 'Amor! Amor!' Here were the bars and the talking men, the smell of sweet coñac and old dry sherries. A clear cold air, churches and oranges, and a lean-faced generation moving against white walls in sharp silhouettes of scarlet and black. It did not take more than five minutes to wipe out fifteen years and to return me whole to this thorn-cruel, threadbare world, sombre with dead and dying Christs, brassy with glittering Virgins.

We took a room in a hotel which stood close to the harbour's edge, high above the masts of the fishing boats. It was called 'The Queen of the Sea', and its walls were faced with the wave-blue tiles of Seville. Its dining-room was a patio of pillars standing under a green-glass roof, and its green furniture was hand-painted with roses, hunting dogs and bulls. The proprietor was a swarthy Moor, morose, fat-necked, with a Farouk-like paunch. He spent his days chewing cold fat pork and playing glum games with the cash register. Ramón, the manager, who was quiet and courtly, had a long dark face of extreme nobility and torment. The rest of the staff included six chambermaids, four waiters, three kitchen-maids, two washer women, a clerk, a cook, a pageboy, a night-watchman and a turnkey. Yet this hotel was one of the cheapest in the town.

We soon settled in and the place served us well. It was an active, busy inn. The rooms were full of coughs, groans, cries and laughter; the stairways full of the songs of chambermaids, and the beds full of fleas – the progenitors of long exhausted dreams. But the food was plentiful. Our first meal, served at half-past two that afternoon, offered us olives, sardines, shellfish, prawns, a large dish of rice served with meat and saffron, flan and fruit, and a bottle of wine fetched in for a shilling.

After such a meal, drenched in the green, brutish, stimulating oils of the hills, there was nothing one could do. So we climbed to our room overlooking the bay and lay in a lethargy till five o'clock while the girls in the sewing-room above sat singing the languorous songs of their villages.

At five o'clock there was a new awakening. The café tables on the pavement below began to fill up with the customers of the evening. Waiters ran to and fro with prawns and manzanilla. Minstrels struck up on guitars and mandolines. There also arrived an army of touts and merchants—shoeblacks, newsboys, lottery-ticket sellers, gypsies with charms, boys with combs and postcards, women with baskets of cakes and sweets. Among the throbbing chords of the musicians arose their high-pitched cries: 'Ay, carne membrillo!', 'Ay, dulces buenas!', 'Limpia! Limpia!'; 'Africa de hoy!' It was time to be up and about.

So I went forth into the town and tried to reacquaint myself with the pattern of it. But of course it was not the same at all. My memory, over the years, had torn the old town down, rebuilt it, laid out the streets in quite different order and obliterated some of their most dominating landmarks. In that time I also had been torn down, rebuilt and had many landmarks

obliterated. The town, after all, remained the truth, and I the
shifting fable.

I struck up through the narrow streets that I could not remember and that remembered me not. Yet here were the same
square, gold-roofed houses with their grilled mysterious windows, the same delicate clusters of ironwork clamped to the
warm white walls, the same bougainvilia and morning glory
stretching forth their membranes of blue and purple over all.
There was the same harsh singing in the patios, the same snap
of wit in the air, the same smells of oil, of wine and charcoal, of
raw fish and the raw sea.

Those years ago I had walked in from Càdiz, with my violin
on my back, and lodged at the old inn of San Antonio – where I
used to pay threepence a night to lie on a sack of straw in the
courtyard. I went now and found the place. Mules and tasselled
harness and blue-painted wagons still crowded the courtyard.
Carters and their families crouched on the cobbles cooking up
soup on little braziers. Wine-skins hung from the walls, and the
corners groped with echoes. But the old proprietor was dead,
and the hunchback porter was dead, and María the maid had
flown with a Moor, and nobody would believe, looking at my
English tweeds, that I had ever been there at all.

Yet this was where I met Pedro from the Asturias, and Ciego
the blind globe-trotter from Lisbon, and we had gone into seedy
partnership. We used to swim by night in the bay, and fill sand-
wiches with sea-urchins and stuff them into the pockets of sleeping policemen. Ciego was the beggar, Pedro the thief, and for
myself I lived how I could. Each night we would pool our
money, buy fish and wine, and then go off and serenade the
nuns. After that we all slept side by side among the mules. I
stood looking now at the rough cobbles where once we lay, the
hollows that fitted our hips, the mangers where we hung our
clothes. And the new proprietor stood looking at me, smiling
his disbelief, and there was nothing to show that we had ever
been there. Pedro had died in jail. The Ciego, after living some

time in happy darkness, had walked into the sea on a drunken night. And here was I in a new tweed suit.

So I left the inn of San Antonio, and went up to the plaza and sat down at a café table and put away the old town and prepared to accept the real one I saw around me. In the late afternoon sun it glowed slumberous and golden. Palm trees exploded darkly overhead, and orange trees bore fruit and blossom both together, giving out mixed odours of spring and Christmas. On the broad pavement below the palms, scarlet-skirted little girls skipped in haloes of honeyed dust. And by the fountain, posing for an old frock-coated photographer, stood several small boys in new confirmation suits, white, waxen, stiff and holy.

At the café tables around me four students, their heads together like card-players, were reciting poems to each other. At another table two girls were painfully composing a letter. At a third sat a young man all alone, weeping softly and eating nuts.

But such is the open market of Mediterranean life that I was not long left in doubt about any of them. The students, raising their voices in a climax of rhetorical extravagance, proved to be engaged in creating extemporaneous odes in honour of the local football team. The girls, catching my eye, said I looked like a scholar and would I help them with their letter, which was a declaration of love to a soldier in Morocco. And the solitary young man, looking at no one, suddenly struck the table and cried out to all the world: 'I have no taste to get married! And why should I? I promised her nothing. I only took her to a pastry shop. . .'

And he continued to weep, not hiding his grief at all.

Night in the town. The shops still glow. One walks through thick crowds which the day's end has called forth into the streets, a multitude which flows down the hill towards the harbour, giving off, as it goes, a remorseless pebbly chatter like the drag of a stream in flood. Here, during the late hours before the evening meal, the whole town passes before one. Here, in the dim patches of light thrown forth from the doors of wine-shops, one sees the great eyes of the girls, formal as Persian paintings, and brick-red mouths and bodies loose as dancers'. And the young men, wickedly handsome, with thick greased hair and curling moustaches, each face a gypsy's warning, each jacket slung like a cape over the swaggering shoulder. These boys were made for quartered hose, for Toledo swords and quick flashing brawls of honour. But today their claws are clipped and rhetoric their only weapon.

At this time, too, pass all the other characters of the Spanish streets: the dark veiled women hurrying home from the priest; the Civil Guard whom nobody greets; gold-skinned sailors and strutting carters; goat-faced ruffians down from the hills; and old men with the hollow eyes of hermits, their skin stretched thin on chill ascetic bones. Then come the merry, dirt-grained beggar children, aping the professional whine but giggling helplessly behind it; and the cripples crawling on hands and knees; the curious idiots waltzing and singing in long tattered cloaks; and the ghostly blind, with their lottery tickets, stalking obliviously through the crowds, calling their numbers like mystic incantations, their white eyes fixed on the empty sky.

So the first night in Spain wore itself out. For hours I watched and wandered, feeling the hot ground under my feet, hearing again the broken lazy dialect of Andalusia, and seeing in the faces around me the dark, unconquered countenances of the Moors. At twopence a glass I drank white wine, sharp and strong as the cheese of a goat. Then I walked back down to the harbour, mazed and unsteady, and the lights of Gibraltar poured out of the sky like a heap of diamonds on the flat dark sea.

It was late now and the harbour was deserted. Café chairs were piled up on the pavements and a watchman slept on the stones. All was dim light and shadows and a lapping of invisible water. Suddenly, from a dark doorway, a figure appeared and blocked my path, a young man with fierce slit-eyes and a crumbling pock-marked face. Stealthily he rolled up the sleeves of his

American flying-jacket and I saw that his naked arms were strapped to the elbows with watches.

'You wan' good Swiss?' he said hurriedly. 'You wan' Park-air Fifty-one? Come on, fella. Cost you nothin'. Is very cheap. Is contrabando.'

I paused to take him in. Meanwhile, he kept edging away, looking quickly to right and to left, like a wild animal at a water-hole, too nervous to drink.

Ah, contrabando. Sweet fruit of Algeciras. I dodged behind him and slipped into my hotel. I was back indeed, and there was a loud ticking in my ears.

In our hotel we were soon part of the furniture, polished each day by the curious courtesies of the staff. Ramón, the manager, revealed from behind his brooding face a quiet almost tender sense of humour. At dinner the next night he gave me a cigarette – a cheap, strong local brand tasting of tar and feathers.

'We call them "forget-me-nots", he said. 'If you forget them – they go out.'

'I'll never forget this one,' I said, and he laughed from his throat like a laugh from a tomb.

Manolo, our waiter, on the other hand, never laughed at all. He was a young man of about twenty-two, with a small thin body and a long large head, which made him look as though he had been carved for a cathedral niche. He had beautiful eye-lashes and dark wet eyes that seemed to be focused perpetually upon some distant vista of voluptuous melancholy.

He served each meal as though he were serving Mass, with many little bows and elaborate flourishes of the napkin. He always brought me the fattest prawns, because he knew I liked them. And on the second night, without a word of warning and with only the slightest of smiles on his curved lips, he presented me with a poem.

It was written out in immaculate copperplate handwriting such as I have never seen before, except on a five-pound note.

There were about thirty lines to the poem, and its subject was love. I read it through in silence, while Manolo rocked gently on his heels, his head on one side, like a waiter who waits for a client to pronounce on a sauce. At last I asked him where he got it.

'It is mine,' he said. 'I am a poet. I wrote it but yesterday at a late hour of the night. It is beautiful.'

I agreed that it was so, and I said that it was full of fine thoughts, too. And that was enough for Manolo. From then on he brought me a new poem every day. At the hotel he worked continuously from eleven in the morning to twelve o'clock at night. Yet every morning there was a new poem laid out on my table beautifully inscribed in that flowing hand. There were poems to God, to his boy friend, to anxiety, to the Catholic Kings, to anarchy, and to 'our unquiet love'.

'What inspiration,' I said at last.

'It is sensibility,' he answered simply. 'I have much of it.'

We no longer professed any interest in food; our conversations assumed a higher plane. Previously, Manolo had been in the habit of gliding up to our table and inclining his mouth to my ear to warn me about the fish or the rice. Now, approaching me in the same confidential manner, he would whisper hoarsely: 'Love is an earthquake of happiness, of which the heart is the epicentre.' Or 'What is Youth save Hope? What is Age except Regret?' Following such pronouncements he would cock his head sideways for a moment, raise a knowing black eyebrow, then glide without another word back to the service-hatch.

This was provocation, of course, and put me on my mettle, so that in my imperfect Spanish I wrestled with epigrams to astonish him also. There followed days in which we never met without exchanging pensamientos in hushed, grave tones. 'God is a fable writ in holy water,' he would whisper, passing me with a bowl of soup. I would savour this with a low 'Ah!', and we would nod solemnly to each other, then go on about our business. Presently, on my way out into the street, I might find him standing by the door, taking a breath of air. He would draw back, bowing slightly. 'Love's dart is like a mosquito,' I would hiss in his ear, 'for both engender fever.' At this his body would stiffen for a moment, struck still with the truth of my words, then he would shake his head and sigh heavily, giving me a look of professional admiration. For Manolo, flicking the dishes with his butterfly napkin, or gazing blindly at the ceiling with his melting eyes, was, at all times, a professional indeed.

On another night we went out to the 'Street of the Two Brothers', to a wine cave that had attracted us by its shabby look and by the merry sounds we heard coming from within. The place was nothing more than a low-arched drinking tunnel, full of fishermen, dim lights and flickering gothic shadows. There were no glass-topped tables here, no cubist mirrors, paper flowers, brass barmaids and chromium-plated pin-tables. The tavern was stripped down to the bare boards of good fellowship – a whitewashed wall, a rough wooden bar, wine in great vats and men in tempestuous good humour.

We entered to the cry of a fisherman singing an ecstatic fandango that shivered the roots of one's hair. The singer, who was leaning against a huge sweating barrel of amontillado, was a short wiry little man, scrub-haired, swarthy faced, with a profile from Egypt. He wore a blue jersey and torn linen trousers, and he was surrounded by a rapt group of friends whose shining weather-beaten faces were creased in the very excesses of pleasure.

We drank black wine at sixpence a bottle and listened to him. He stood there stiffly, his eyes closed, his dark face raised to the light, singing with a powerful controlled passion that shook his whole body through. At the beginning of each verse his limbs convulsed, as though gathering their strength; and at the end he reached such shuddering paroxysms of intricate invention that the whole room roared with praise. He sang through the nose, with the high-pitched cry of Africa, and he sang with the most natural grief and happiness, varying the words with little phrases of his own full of sly wickedness and tragic beauty.

They told me his name was Pepe, and that he came from Huelva, the old Phoenician port east of Cadiz. And from the look of his sharp dark face and slanting eyes, remote as a buried mask, he might easily have been one of the founders of that city. He looked as though he had landed that day from a voyage that began five thousand years before. And he sang – making up the words as he went along – of boats and storms, of saints and monsters, of mysterious longings and mysterious loves. He sang, too, a saetas I shall never forget, a savage impromptu of adoration to the Virgin, harsh, scalp-raising, and accompanied by sonorous drum-beats on an empty barrel.

As the evening wore on, and more wine was drunk, Pepe grew more and more excited. He seized a straw hat and a broom and became a most agile clown. With rolling eyes and a perfectly controlled body he aped the Civil Governor and the Governor's wife, a crab caught in a trap, the soldiers of Napoleon, and the 'Due de Vellinton'. The last two, brushing aside a hundred and fifty years with a few superb gestures, brought down the house as though they were the most topical of jokes.

Flushed with triumph now, Pepe looked round the bar seeking for further inspiration, and his eyes fell on Kati. She was the only woman there. He snatched off his hat and pressed it to his heart, then advanced towards me, and bowed.

'With your permission,' he said, 'I am you.'

He stood close beside me and turned towards Kati; and with hands and body and fluid voice sang immediate love-songs right into her eyes. From then on, Pepe and I were drinking out of the same bottle. He was I. His arm was about my shoulder. 'With your permission,' he said, and began a new verse. He reeked of wine and olives, of garlic and the sea. He reeked also of glory. And he looked into Kati's eyes and sang songs of such touching tenderness and grace, such delicate perfection, that I grieve that I can no longer remember them.

I loved that man, and envied him. He inhabited still the pure sources of feeling that once animated us all. For us, of course, they are increasingly clogged by each new triumph of enlightenment and comfort. But for Pepe, and for many others like him in Spain, they are still preserved by the paradoxes of poverty, illiteracy, bad roads and the great silences of the mountains and the sea.

Later that evening I walked the streets alone, too bright with wine to feel the need of sleep. There was a curious music in the air and a stamping of feet in the darkness, and as I stood in the plaza an army of young men suddenly appeared and came marching towards me, singing lustily. They were bearing guitars, mandolines, cymbals, flutes and drums of pigskin which growled when you stroked them. 'We are going to a wedding,' cried the leader, and invited me to go with them. Very glad of a wedding on such a night, I accepted without hesitation. I was given a pigskin drum to stroke, and I fell in behind, and we all marched away to the fishermen's suburb, playing loudly as we went.

It was a warm, dark winter night and the season for serenading was in full swing. On every hand the town was alive with it. Women and children leaned out of rose-red windows to watch us as we passed by. We began to meet other bands marching and counter-marching about the town. Sometimes they crossed our paths with hideous discord and then just faded away into the darkness. At others, they met us head on in narrow streets, and no one would give way, and then what stiff-necked rivalry there was, what tightening of strings and jutting of jaws, what glorious bedlam as we all stood breast to breast, sweating and thumping our instruments and each trying to outplay the other.

We left the town at last, and climbed the high ground above the harbour, the wind in our teeth, the lights far below us, and the young men arguing all the way. We reached the fishermen's suburb, where the wedding was, and halted, with some ceremony, outside a darkened house. Here we banged on the door, struck warning chords, shouted and kicked the walls. At first nothing happened; then a grey old man, roused from his sleep, poked his head from a window and cursed us all roundly. We had come, it seemed, to the wrong house.

Then we found, at last, the wedding-party, and were welcomed with cheers and wine. Here was a crowded room full of sweating girls, clambering children, and stiff old ladies as black and brittle as charcoal. There were pieces of ham handed round on toothpicks, Gibraltar biscuits and Tangier sweets, speeches, introductions, song and dance, and a beaming bride and a scratching groom.

The band placed itself in the middle of the room and played a programme of martial music well nigh drowned by the pigskin drums. The walls of the little room seemed to bend outwards with noise, the children screamed, the girls cowered in the corners, and the sweat ran down from the ceiling. Then, after more drink, ham and speeches, enthusiasm waned, and we were shown the street.

Here we paused for a while in argument, for there was still work to be done. Where now should we go and who else should we honour? Girls' names were proposed, attacked, fought for, won or abandoned. And such names they were on the Spanish air, exotic, round, baroque and many-flavoured, a litany of virtues, a calendar of saints. Finally we accepted six of them, those best loved by the loudest in the band, and set off to serenade them.

It was now about two o'clock in the morning. Other grunting bands still marched about the town. We trailed over waste ground, under bridges, along railway lines, through darkened squares. From time to time we paused under a window, banged on a door, and struck up a military march. Sometimes we were ignored. Sometimes a sleepy girl would drag herself from her warm bed, lean drowsily over the balcony, and scratch and yawn good-naturedly in our faces. When this happened one of us would detach himself. Quick, then, were the words of love whispered up from the street, while the rest of the band, for a discreet moment, stood silently aside. Then, with a crash of chords and a growl of the pigskins, we were off again to the next. Until the light of dawn we proceeded thus. The serenading season had begun indeed, and few virgins in the town got much sleep that night. Very few of the rest of us either. And for days my fingers were sore from those pigskin drums.

One stormy but invigorating morning we set out to walk to Tarifa, the old Arab town lying twelve miles along the coast in the direction of Càdiz. Armed with coñac against the cold, we climbed slowly into the mountains, while a stiff wind blew in from the Atlantic bearing strong salt smells of northern weather. Ahead of us lay the Sierra of the Moon and on our left the Sierra of Gazelles, high and dark, shrouded with storms and eagles.

It was a morning of mysterious monotones; black rocks above and a blacker sea beneath. We saw one little girl burning leaves by the side of the road and an old man whipping acorns out of a tree. We saw the smoke of a charcoal burner blowing raggedly out of the cork forest and heard the crack of a rifle down in a ravine. Otherwise we were alone in the world, save for the eagles that dropped out of the crags to look at us.

This coast road winds through iron-coloured rocks to a mountain pass above Tarifa, and for two hours we saw no sign of traffic on it. Then a farmer in a mule-cart came rattling out of a field, and, seeing us toiling over the stones, he stopped and offered us a lift. We climbed to the top of a load of potatoes and sat beside him. He was a fat and bristly fellow, with a waistband of broad black silk in which he stored tobacco, cheese and olives for the journey. All this he shared with us, and as we went he talked comfortably about his affairs.

He was once, it seemed, a great landowner hereabouts, possessing twelve farms and twelve sons, all famous and worth much gold. Then four of the farms were lost in a lawsuit, and four of the sons in the Civil War. But that was not the end of him. There was still a son for each remaining farm, and he was master of them all. He was a big farmer, he said, and grew everything. There were potatoes here, cork trees farther on, maize down by the mad-house, and olives in the valley of toads. There was also a garden for tomatoes, an onion patch, a mill, a vineyard and a ruined chapel full of fattened pigs.

'Buy land and breed sons,' he said, 'and you can't go wrong. Come war and thieves and ruined harvests – they don't signify at all.' He thumped himself hard in the loins. 'If a man's got strong blood, like me, and scatters his seed wide enough, that man must flourish. Such is the truth and I tell it to you.'

So we continued, in the greatest satisfaction, till we came down at last out of the hills to the white town jutting on the sea. The farmer left us here and drove on into the farther country, and we turned towards Tarifa and stood below the walls.

This town, small as a village, is the most southerly point in Europe, yet the air it wears is not of Europe at all. We approached the narrow Moorish gateway, where the road runs through the walls. 'Most royal, most loyal city of Tarifa', it said, on coloured tiles above. For this coastal stronghold, built for Islam, was recaptured and held by Spain long before the Moors were driven out of Europe. So it stood for years among the alien spears, a scene of bloody sieges, betrayal and massacre. But it remained the outpost of the Catholic Kings and never again surrendered.

We passed through the gateway and into the city, and the sun broke through and shone. Tarifa, within the walls, was packed as tight as a box of bricks. But the small square houses, decorated with delicate ironwork and built round tiny flowering patios, gave an impression of miniature spaciousness, a garden enclosed, an ancient perfection preserved in poverty and love.

For Tarifa was quite obviously poor. Once a name of terror in the Straits, a nest for the sea-raiders who once dominated these waters, the city lies harmless now like a wrecked and gilded barge. But the gilt is fresh, and flowers hang bright from the balconies, and the air in the streets has the clean golden silence of perpetual afternoon.

Most Spanish towns are lapped with noise, with wagons and motor-horns, donkeys and tinkers, and the ceaseless clamour of café conversation. But here there was an almost unearthly silence, cool and becalmed, a silence of no time. We threaded around the narrow cobbled alleys, and small dogs slept in shadows as though bred only for sleep. A few brown girls stood motionless by a fountain, unspeaking, stilled with secrets. A few dark men stole quietly through archways and disappeared into the profound gloom of shuttered patios. A few dark eyes watched us through the grilles of windows. And a solitary beggar girl, with huge dumb eyes, followed us slowly with a smile.

I felt we had stepped aside from all the activity of the earth and entered a charmed and voiceless world, a world where people lived as hushed as plants, taking their life from the sun without a sound. The Spanish kings may well have recovered this town in 1392, but Tarifa remained almost mystically oriental, the women wore veils of silence, and the men walked cloaked in shadow and the sun.

Down a narrow street, near an empty plaza, we ate our midday meal. The beggar child watched us through the window for a while, then, picking up a piece of charcoal from the road, began to draw pictures on the white wall opposite. She drew an ass, a lion and a tree full of birds. When we had finished our meal she came and took us by the hand and led us to them.

As we fingered the birds and stroked the lion's mane she gazed up at us with great eyes swimming in shadows.

'What would you like best in all the world?' I asked.

'To sail a ship in the night,' she answered.

'And where would you go?'

'Away, to find my father.'

She came with us down to the seashore, and we sat together

on the white sands, eating oranges and pastries and watching the long rollers coming in from the Bermudas.

Then we said good-bye and walked out of the town and got a lift in a motor-car back to Algeciras. As we returned through the stormy mountains, a gale blowing now and rain coming on, our driver, who was a horse-doctor, spoke passionately about the loss of Gibraltar, but he said that Churchill was a good man and might hand it back to Spain any day now.

During the days that followed, a raging storm blew up out of the Straits, accompanied by a harsh east wind. Gibraltar Rock, trailing a perpetual plume of cloud, looked like a stricken battle-ship on fire. The bay leapt and seethed with green and milky waves. The fishermen crouched miserably in doorways, watching their boats as parents watch sick children. And the Civil Guards drew cloaks over their noses and flapped about like wounded birds.

Rafael, the page-boy, ran in and out of the hotel with doom on his face, his proud new uniform shrinking rapidly.

'Ay! Ay!' he moaned. 'What wind! What tempest!'

I asked him if this was usual weather.

'Rare as a green dog,' he said, shaking himself.

It meant an end to all normal life in the town. No boats would put out, so there was a lack of fresh fish. No one would go into the streets if they could help it, and those who must stole aw-fully about, wrapped up to the eyes with scarves as though the wind spelt plague. Another consequence of the storm was the glut of stranded travellers in the hotel. There was no way across the Straits save by the Algeciras ferries, and all travellers by train from Europe to Morocco came here to catch these boats. But with such seas running the boats refused to sail.

Suddenly, therefore, the bars and dining-rooms of the hotel were full of the lost and surprised from all over Europe. They sat around all day, staring at the walls, nibbling nuts and waiting for deliverance. Unprepared as they were for more than an hour

in Algeciras, the delay seemed to rob them of all power to ex-
press themselves, and the waiters kept running to me in despair
to ask the French for flan, the German for banana, or the English for soft-boiled eggs.

There was a wide variety among the travellers: a Huguenot
hotel-keeper from Dublin, going to Tangier for his blood-
pressure; a poor American painter with his French-Arab wife;
three caravaning Swedes; a Norwegian-American and her two
blonde daughters; an ex-sailor from Alamos in trouble with the
police; and a thin, pale, pendantic young civil servant from the
Channel Islands.

The effects of the delay upon them were also various, and at
times quite startling. The Huguenot hotel-keeper drank brandy
all day long and blew up paper bags to test his wind. The Nor-
wegian and her daughters tiptoed in shocked horror about the
passages, pale and martyred by the plumbing. One of the
Swedes, in gritty English, made love to the sailor and was pun-
ched on the nose. And the American painter, in bad French, sat
quarrelling with his wife over the works of Donatello, striking
the table every so often and crying out to the amazed fishermen: 'Jeeze, ain't she dumb though? She jus' don't know from
Harry! Good ker-ripes!'

But the prim young man from the Channel Islands was probably in a worse state than any of them. He was making a rapid
tour of France, Spain and Morocco, every stage of which he had
worked out beforehand to the split second. Delay was calamity.
For two miserable days he sat in the hall, checking his time-
tables, making nervous calculations in his notebook, looking at
the clock, and clucking. For two days he would not eat, because
eating in Algeciras was not included in his itinerary. The second
evening we forced him to have dinner with us, and afterwards
to try some coñac. Quite soon, in a kind of white-faced despera-
tion, growing more and more formal, he grew more and more
drunk. In the end, speaking with Whitehall precision, he broke
down altogether.

'In my position,' he said, 'as Assistant to the Postmaster, I am assured ... of an adequate salary. And later, of course ... of a pension ... concomitant with my grade. And yet ... The tears streamed down his face. 'What does it all mean? I would like to be famous, my name to be remembered. But how? I ask, but how?'

We picked him up – and his time-table – off the floor, and put them both to bed.

Among others stranded in the port were several shaggy groups of yachtsmen – British, French and Italian. One met them in the bars at night, a false-faced lot, all drinking heavily, all wearing braided caps. The French and Italians looked like film extras, with an anxious shiftiness about them as theatrical as grease-paint. The British included young men with polar beards, middle-aged captains with flaring faces and half-drowned eyes, and several ageless girls whom the captains always introduced as their pursers. They were quarrelsome and intensely suspicious of each other, and although they seemed to hang together, the presence of a stranger revealed some queer cracks in their solid-arity.

A young man would lead me darkly aside. 'You want gin?' he'd say. 'Loads of it aboard. You sell it, and we'll go fifty-fifty. Have to hit the old man on the head though. He keeps the key, the sot.'

A girl would lead me to another corner. 'You don't know what I've been through,' she'd whisper hoarsely. 'He nearly pushed me overboard in the Bay. Said it was an accident, but I wouldn't put it past him. Never did trust the swine. Wish I'd stayed in Rep.'

From time to time there would be high words, blows, tears and sentimental reconciliations. Then the skipper, drinking rum, would embrace everyone. 'I got the best crew in the world,' he'd say. 'They love me like a dad.' Then there were nods, winks, obscure allusions, expressing a sense of shared mission, secret and dangerous. They were a shabby lot, but they all seemed to have plenty of money, to be bound on long mysterious voyages, and yet to have been stuck in the Straits for months. There was no doubt at all about it. Something more than the pure call of the sea had brought them to these waters.

Across the bay stood rich Gibraltar. Across the Straits the free port of Tangiers. For the forbidden goods they had to offer, Spain was starved. So the yachts and fishing-boats ran to and fro on the dark nights, and Algeciras was their clearing-house. Watches, fountain-pens, nylons, cigarettes, sweets, cocoa and canned meats: here, in this town, I could buy them any day, untaxed and hot from the smugglers' hands.

The organization was smooth but implacable, and the right form of bribe had always to be observed. One morning, as I was dressing, I heard the crack of a rifle, and looking out of the window saw a young man spread-eagled on the pavement below. 'A contrabandista,' said the chambermaid, shaking out the sheets. But he was only a poor workman, a lone hand who had failed to obey the rules. So the green-cloaked policemen dumped his body in a cart and wheeled him like rubbish away.

But in crowded Algeciras hundreds of other young men stood around in the streets all day. They were not fishermen, or labourers, and their pockets were stuffed with American cigarettes. Every morning an army of thousands – cooks and washerwomen, ostlers, dockers, roadmen, waiters, gardeners and guides – went across to Gibraltar to work. Every evening back they came, bulging like clowns with their loot. So they and their wives drank rich cocoa on cold nights, and their daughters wore stockings of silk, and the children sometimes ate chocolate. Nowhere else in Spain were these things either seen or tasted, at least not by the poor.

Gibraltar, that juicy pear-drop of rock hanging from dry Spain's southern tip, was captured by the British some two and a half centuries ago. Many of the original Spanish inhabitants fled to the mainland, and most of them settled in this town.

Never, never did they cease to grieve their loss and shame. And yet . . .

'Do you know what the people of Algeciras are called?' asked Ramón, handing me some chewing-gum. 'Los Especiales – the favoured ones. They talk a lot about "our Gibraltar" and "the Spanish Rock". They cry and stick out their teeth. But I'll tell you something.' He paused, and laid a finger along his nose. 'They wouldn't have it back for the world, you know. It would be the ruin of them.'

2. Choirs and Bulls - Seville

In an afternoon of gale and storm we left Algeciras and took the motor-bus for Seville, a hundred miles to the north. Africa and the Straits had disappeared in a driving whirl of cloud and the sky was the colour of octopus ink. Our road was a bad one, narrow, cratered and steep, and it took us straight up into the Sierra de los Gazules, a dark region of craggy forests where no birds sing.

From a distance these mountains look like a herd of driven animals, lean, diseased and beaten to the bone. Near at hand they revealed a shuttered, oppressed world, particularly so this stormy day, under its heavy sky. There was something about the streaming rocks and wet, lead-coloured trees that gave one a sense of unnatural freedoms, of a desolate secret life. Indeed, as one expected, it was a place of bandits; and we had two Civil Guards, fully armed, riding with us for our protection.

These two did not impress us, however. They were green, sick-looking youths and they rode with an air of misery. As we bumped up the rocky forest road they crouched low and peered anxiously out of the windows, while yellow home-made cigarettes hung wet from their loose lips. They were here on sufferance of course, and they knew it. For the bandits were as indigenous to these parts as the wild boar and stag, and when they struck they did so with the fine assurance of those who are indulging an ancient privilege. Moreover, their ranks had been stiffened of late by an influx of escaped prisoners and political outlaws. Oh, yes, they were bad men, said a neighbour, hugging his fat lap. Along this very road, this very winter, several unhappy travellers had been shamefully murdered. It was a natural peril of the mountains. But the señores were not to fear; the Civil Guards were valiant, and the bandits never attacked foreigners anyway, it was not their custom.

On this occasion, somewhat to our disappointment, we were not attacked at all. It was not bandit weather; and we did not see so much as a living creature in all those mountains. When at last we came out of them and descended into the plain, the Civil Guards said how lucky we were, and we said how lucky they were, and in an atmosphere of mutual congratulation they left us and took another bus back to the coast.

The storm here left us also. As neat as a ruled line drawn across the sky, the black clouds ended and radiant blue began. We came to Alcalá de los Gazules, a terraced town of bright white houses hung with red flowers and roofed with gold. White pigeons floated like thistledown in the sky above, and sunshine came off the walls with the force of an electric flare. We stopped here, and sat by the roadside, drinking wine and screwing up our eyes.

Later we began to cross the plain that rolls gently towards the Guadalquivir. It was brown as a camel and smelt of fine herbs. There were walled farms here and there, and wooden crosses by the roadside; herds of black bulls roamed slowly in bronze pastures, a castle stood up sharply from the cone of a dead volcano, and above, in the wide sky, two white flamingos flew.

The day set fair, and the Sierras receded like a distant battle, dropping low on the distant horizon in a torment of rock and cloud. Our bus driver was a cautious man and maintained a humble speed. We bucked through craters, and swerved round wandering cattle, and by late afternoon approached the fortress town of Medina Sidonia whose Duke once led a fleet to capture Britain. The town stood now, stark on its weathered rock, wrecked like a galleon decaying in the sun. We circled it slowly, and picked up a few survivors, and by dusk had arrived among the ornate villas and pungent wine smells of Jerez de la Frontera.

The worst part of our journey was over. We had come a long and brutish road, taking over four hours to travel sixty miles. Now, in the dark, we ran smoothly up the Guadalquivir valley. The driver switched on Radio Sevilla, and sang to it, and by nine o'clock we arrived among the spread lights of that city.

We entered Seville in style, leaving the bus station through a double row of porters, cab-drivers and hotel-touts all drawn up to greet us. As we walked down between their ranks we were assailed by cries of welcome, admiration, promises and advice, names of hotels and details of food and beds.

We lost our nerve, and picked a man at random, and drove off with him to a hotel of some class, though moderately priced. After supper we went out into the streets, which were still light and gay, and full of people, in spite of the late hour. Old men sat in the wide windows of their clubs watching the girls go by. Taverns and bars threw open their doors to us, and the windows of the shops were packed with pretty emblems of the city – tambourines, castanets, embroidered shawls, flamenco dolls, holy images and glittering chandeliers.

The effect of such tinselled knick-knacks, displayed with such bright assurance, acts as an immediate aphrodisiac upon the senses. The effervescence in the streets, the floating music, the flowers and towers and azulejos and orientalisms are part of it too. In no time the city has one in thrall. It is all part of the special femininity of Seville, a mixture of gaiety and languor. For among so much that is harsh and puritan in this country, Seville is set apart like a mistress, pampered and adored. It is the heart of Andalusia, and of the Andalusians. It is the first charge on their purse and passions. In spite of war, hunger, decay and cruelty, ways are still found to preserve the softer bloom of this city, its charm and professional alegría Not only in its own province, but throughout all Spain, men turn to Seville as a symbol ; it is the psyche of their genius, the coil that regenerates their sharpest pleasures and instincts. The miner from the Asturias and the fisherman from Cartagena, though never having set foot in it, will speak of the city with jealousy and love. So Seville remains, favoured and sensual, exuding from the banks of its golden river a miasma of perpetual excitement, compounded of those appetites that are most particularly Spanish – chivalry, bloodshed, poetry and religious mortification.

Thus one sees, often in the meanest streets, the ritual furniture that builds up the myth, the cracked walls dressed with green-leafed flowers, the watered patios whispering with tiny fountains, the writhing Christs and brooding Virgins lit by perpetual lamps. One sees the ragged schoolgirls dancing in gutters, intense and sexual, weaving their hands like snakes ; sees the doomed bull-fighter kneeling at Mass, hears the death-shout in the Ring, and bursts of superb singing in the night.

Seville of sweet wines and bitter oranges, of dandy horsemen bearing their girls to the parks, of fantastic villas and radiant whores, of finery, filth and interminable fiesta centred around the huge dead-weight of the cathedral: this is the city where, more than in any other, one may bite on the air and taste the multitudinous flavours of Spain – acid, sugary, intoxicating, sickening, but flavours which, above all in a synthetic world, are real as nowhere else.

The next day, after a breakfast of coffee and caraway buns, we walked through a litter of leaves and orange blossom to a street market near the University. Here, laid out along the sidewalks in a delirium of rust, was all the precious debris of a people who never throw anything away. Un-American, non-productive, mechanical innocents that they are, they would treasure the last thread of a boot-lace. And here, arranged like jewels, in formal patterns on the ground, were old nails, bent screws, broken files, battered buckets, tangled wire, rods of iron and bunches of huge medieval keys. Nothing was despised and everything had a price. Sharp-eyed customers raked and sorted, tapped and bit, and rang things on the ground. And as much shrewd argument went into a purchase here as one might see in the diamond markets of Amsterdam.

Farther on were stalls of slightly better-class goods: plaster dogs, single boots, oil-lamps, singing birds, flowers and gramophones with horns. There was also a large collection of Madrid-made hand-mirrors which rippled one's image like running water. From all this happy rubbish I bought a rose for two-pence, and for five shillings a small bronze Christ, cadaverous, pain-wracked and unbelievably old.

Leaving the market we walked by the Moorish Wall and got caught up in a demonstration of students who were bound for the Town Hall to demand a free holiday. They were dressed, for some reason, in black sixteenth-century doublets and hose, and they carried heraldic banners. But it was a bright sweet day, fresh from a night of rain, so we hired an open carriage and drove to the Park of María Luisa. Seedy, fly-blown, with creaking wheels – but what elegance such motion has. Except for being borne in a hand-litter I cannot imagine a better. The long-maned pony gently trotted, the coachman flicked a languid whip, and smoothly we went through the Delicious Gardens, while blossoming trees floated past our heads like slow, green-scented clouds.

The park was formal yet flouncy, like the dress of an Edwardian beauty. The air was soft and spring-like. Children in large hats and long white pinafores bowled their grave hoops among the rose trees. Black-stockinged girls bent over pools, poking at goldfish with the stems of lilies. And opulent mammas, ripe in black satin, drowsed at their ease on the blue-tiled benches. It was a landscape by Renoir or Steer, an end-of-the-century dream; and as we clopped our way along, smelling the oranges and roses and passing the lacy girls posed like old postcards among the flower-beds, I felt an unnatural sense of distinction, almost as though I had invented the horse.

So passed the gentle, slumberous afternoon, stopping for

photographs or buying flowers, rolling down avenues of horn-beam and eucalyptus, through tunnels of fresh green, half-dozing to the pony's sighs and the coachman's sonorous snores. Then we came at last to the river-bank, woke up the coachman, paid him off, and set out on foot for Triana.

Triana is Seville's Roman suburb and lies just across the water. It rises flush from the river's edge, a crumbling group of lemon-coloured hovels battered with poverty and age. It is a working place, a suburb of potters, boot-menders and carpenters, with an élite of free-moving mysteriously purposed gypsies. Here are made the shining azulejos which face with blue so many Andalusian villas. Here are made also the painted chairs and glazed images that furnish them. And here are born many of those penniless but inspired exponents of the popular Spanish arts – incomparable guitarists and dancers, feverish poets and small-boned, hot-eyed boys who go early to the bulls, and whose hunger, valour and excesses lead them to swift, unnatural deaths.

We walked among the riverside huts and dwellings, saw an old lady sitting in a doorway chewing dried cod, saw a girl of five dancing solemnly under an old wall, saw a boy fighting a dog with goat horns tied to its head, and heard from the door of a potter's shop the verses of a song which threw up the word 'Triana' over and over again, like a firework.

As we stood on the bridge, in the midst of the muddy river, the sun burnt down slow into the rigging of orange ships, wait-ing the winter harvest. Seville harbour – only a few hundred yards of dock set on the banks of a slow river, fifty miles from the sea, yet once the greatest harbour in the world, and still, in the legends of man, the most important. Columbus, Pizarro and Fernando Magellan, the *Santa María* and the little *Vitoria* – from here they sailed to find a new world, or to be the first in all his-tory to encircle the globe.

On our way back from Triana, up the street of the Catholic

Kings, we looked for a tavern to rest ourselves, and found one called 'Pepito'. It was a lucky chance, for the proprietor was a prodigious epicure, loose-tongued and free-handed. His name was Antonio. He was a bald, youngish man, with a smooth face, shining eyes, stubby ring-covered fingers, and the greasy plumpness that comes from standing long hours behind a bar eating and drinking and waiting for customers. It was his own bar, and he was his own master, and the days were his own to make as pleasant as possible. Seldom, then, did he keep his ringed fingers from picking the food, his fat lips from tasting the many wines of the house. He was an enthusiast, an obsessive, and as soon as we arrived he began to offer us, without charge, glasses of wine from every barrel in the place.

'Approve this,' he would say, banging a new one down on the counter and drawing off a little one for himself. Then, as one drank, he would step back a couple of paces, and stand, head on one side, like a painter observing his canvas. 'You like it? Solera buena. You're right. It's no good. Approve this, then. Oloroso. Very rich. There you are.' And bang came another glass, golden as honey, but set down with such force that half of it jumped out on to the floor. So it went on. For two hours we approved. And for two hours he joined us, glass for glass, sipping holily, watching our eyes while we drank, and telling the history of the wine.

'This is a miracle. Approve the colour. With this you could suckle a baby. So kind it is. With this you could wash the dead and they'd resurrect themselves. Is stupendous, eh?'

And with every new glass Antonio would bawl to his wife, who was hidden behind a screen, and bid her fry some fresh tit-bit to eat with the wine. Great barrels were piled along the walls, chalked in red with their redolent names: Coñac, Manzanilla, Fino, Tinto, Amontillada, Blanca la Casa, Solera and Especial. We had a glass from each barrel, and from the best, several. If one was not emptied before the next was offered it was tossed airily into the street. And with every glass came some new delicious morsel, cooked by the invisible wife; fried fish, fried birds, kidneys, prawns, chopped pork, octopus, beans and sausage.

Antonio was the fat host of a golden age, persuasive, open-fisted, and delighted with our appetites. He cheated himself frivolously for the pleasure of seeing us drink. He talked all the time, and showed us photographs of himself going right back to his mother's breast. And from what we could see the years had hardly changed him at all.

Bewitched by this hospitality, we returned to Antonio another night. We had learned that it was his daughter's birthday, and we brought her cakes. When I placed the parcel on the counter he struck his head with his hand.

'I pollute the house!' he cried, rolling his eyes. 'What sympathy. What grace.' He bawled to his wife, who immediately began frying. Then he shouted upstairs to his daughter, María, to wash her face and put on fresh ribbons and come down and not dishonour him.

'I pollute the house,' he cried again, looking at the cakes in amazement.

His daughter appeared, beautiful and dignified as an infanta, and shook our hands. It was her twelfth birthday. She talked to us solemnly about geography and arithmetic, while her father ripped out the corks of special bottles, prised open tins of ham and tunny fish, sent out for cigars, and spread the whole feast before us. And thus we gorged together till after midnight. Antonio was in a frenzy of pleasure, drunk with generosity, riotous and noisy as though at a wedding. María remained cool, courtly, soft spoken and rather prim. But the wife, endlessly frying behind the screen, never appeared at all.

Most cities in the world have a particular centre of gravity to which the steps of inhabitants and visitors naturally turn. In London, I suppose, it is Piccadilly. In Seville, without doubt, it is the Cathedral – largest and most non-committal Gothic structure in all Christendom. It is also unlike any other I have ever seen. In contrast to the perpendicular sky-reaching fantasies of England and France, Seville Cathedral is flat and square, a study in the horizontal, almost in prostration, hugging the ground like an encrusted turtle, ponderous with age and veneration. I believe the style owes something to the infidel, for the cathedral was founded upon the site of the great mosque left behind by the Arabs. But within the quadrilateral plan imposed upon it the structure is sternly Gothic, a majestic vastness still humanized by those two surviving Islamic graces : the Court of the Oranges – a scented, shadowy garden – and the magnificent Giralda tower, golden, light and aerial, rising like a delicate rock plant from the heavy Gothic stone.

To this cathedral, on the morning of the Feast of the Immaculate Conception, we went early, and watched the cold red sun throwing stained-glass patterns on the walls. The great interior was a rouged twilight, where the fretted Choir, the candled images and the many gilded dim-lit chapels, presented to the eye the massed details of an intricate sanctity. Though early, the place was busy. The street doors swung continually, dark crowds came and went, small bells tinkled, and incense drifted among the pillars with the sharp blue smell of a winter forest. We saw an old woman on her knees, hobbling from chapel to chapel, intent on some crippling penance. Another held up a child to kiss a Madonna's jewels. We were not in this, nor out of it, but stood like Christian ghosts. A notice, pinned to one of the main doors, caught my eye. It listed, in English, a few brusque rules of behaviour for Protestant tourists, and ended severely : 'Visitors who do not respect these normas will be driven from the Municipal Temple!'

But it was a feast day, and slowly the high altar prepared itself for a visit from the Archbishop. Arm-thick candles were lighted, one by one, and great jewelled stars woke golden in the gloom. The magnificent *retablo* flickered in rich warm light – the living light of wax – which played on the ancient figures of the saints and softened them into a mystery, like visions conjured from smoke. The crowd grew, and an invisible choir coughed and chanted. Then came a procession of scarlet-coated soldiers, trailing long swords. Plump civic dignitaries followed, in morning dress, their chests emblazoned with decorations. All took their places before the altar, and again we waited.

At last, in the centre of a flock of fluttering priests, came the red-capped Archbishop, very old, very slow, loaded with vestments and reverence. Attention, which till then had been fixed upon the glittering face of the altar, upon the stars and haloes which surrounded Christ and the Virgin, now switched to the aged priest. Bent low, he climbed the altar steps, sat himself on a high-backed throne, placed his slippered feet on a gilded footstool, and gave himself up to the complicated ministrations of the serving brethren. In green, gold, scarlet and purple, they massed before him, advanced, retreated, bowed, knelt, touched his robes, kissed his rings and held up the Missal to his trickling eyes. At one moment, four priests eased him gently to his knees, held him in prayer, then restored him to his throne. For the rest he sat like a stiff and ornate doll, without power, it seemed, to command one human gesture – save at the hands of his helpers. So the feast proceeded; the Virgin stood high, remote among the stars; Christ writhed in the flickering shadows; while the rituals revolved more and more about this inert though living image, the Christian Prince of Seville.

We returned several times to the dark echoing spaces of this cathedral, and a week later witnessed the moving ceremony of Las Seises. For hundreds of years on this day in December it has been the custom for a group of young boys to dance and sing on the steps of the high altar for the pleasure of the Virgin. Some say that the occasion reflects the dancing of Samuel before Saul, others that it recalls the boy David. In any case, I doubt whether such a disarming custom could have endured anywhere but in Seville. The boys appeared now, pale and pretty in their miniature elegance, each dressed in fifteenth-century style, with doublets, hose and large cockaded hats. Grave and courtly, they advanced towards the altar, took up their positions on the steps, then moved into a slow and formal dance, weaving chaste patterns like a minuet. They sang, too, in clear innocent harmonies, and their tense, childish movements, revolving beneath the great gaunt images of the altar, were most simple and affecting. Through the years many a Pope has protested against this ceremony, calling it pagan and profane. But none has ever succeeded in suppressing it. For in Seville to dance, even for the Virgin, has never seemed out of place.

Our hotel, just off the main square, was snug, like a tropical hot-house. It had a glass-roofed central well which swam in a perpetual submarine twilight, and on every floor there were potted plants which branched and budded with almost Burmese profusion. Among them sat the innumerable relatives of the proprietor, killing the day-long hours and gazing out through the palm leaves with the unflickering eyes of jungle animals. The place was very clean, and always, somewhere, one saw an old woman scrubbing on her knees.

Paca, our chambermaid, was a beautiful round-faced girl with the ripe dark looks of a Murillo. She was a typical Sevillana, and Murillo, who came from this town, must have seen many like her. Whenever she brought our breakfast in the morning she had the winning habit of entering the shuttered room and awakening us with a soft-sung song. She sang with that warm vocal agility, passionate yet tender, with which every girl in Seville seems naturally born. Her songs were long and sweet, full of regrets and partings, and when her voice in the dark met us half asleep, I lay bemused and could not have wished for a smoother awaking.

Paca earned about thirty-five shillings a month, and she had a lover who was a waiter. She did not know if they would ever get married. She only met him once a week – her single night of freedom. On one such night she came to our room and asked

Kati to help prepare her for the meeting. As she sat on our bed in a tight red frock Kati brushed her long hair and pinned it with a flower. Slowly the drab encrustations of work began to drop from her, her limbs began to stiffen and shine, her great eyes to dilate with dark wet shadows, her head to rise and assume the high carriage of a gypsy. Only for these few hours in every week could she leave the imprisonment of beds and brooms and chamber bells, and walk through the dark lanes as a girl in love. The prospect magnified her beauties like a kiss.

Once we talked with her about the women of other nations and how they compared in looks.

'Chinese women are the most ugly in the world,' said Paca. 'But that is their fault. They are heathens. They do not love God, as we do.'

What about English women? we asked.

'Excuse me,' she said, 'but very ugly. They walk like tired mules, thus' – she rose and slumped across the room, rounding her shoulders, bending her knees – 'and their feet, so large ; and their hair, so short, frizz all round, like scorched straw. And the French – worse, much worse – feísima. And the Germans; fat as pumpkins. But the señorita no' – she turned her glowing eyes on Kati – 'she is most beautiful. All the house are saying so.'

All the house, in fact, were saying that we were not English at all – that we were obviously music-hall artists of unknown origin. It was a delusion which we met often, and was based partly, I think, on Kati's jaunty looks, and partly on the fact that I always wore a fur-lined overcoat and carried two guitars with me everywhere. We did nothing to discourage it : it seemed to bring us certain privileges, and in consequence we were undercharged at restaurants, cosseted at cabarets, entertained freely at taverns and bars, and never expected to have any money.

But to be in Seville without a guitar is like being on ice without skates. So every morning, while Kati went dancing with the Maestro Realito, I took lessons on the instrument in my room.

My instructor, one of Seville's most respected professors of the guitar, was a small sad man, exquisitely polite and patient, poorly but neatly dressed, and addicted to bow-ties made of wallpaper. Each day, at the stroke of ten, he knocked softly at my door and entered on tiptoe, as though into a sick room, carrying his guitar-case like a doctor's bag.

'How are we today?' he would ask sympathetically, 'and how do we proceed?'

Silently, he would place two chairs opposite each other, put me in the one facing the light, sit himself in the other, and then ponder me long and sadly while I played. Infinite compassion, as from one who has seen much suffering, possessed his face while he listened. An expression also of one who, forced to inhabit a solitary peak of perfection, has nowhere to look but downwards at the waste of a fumbling world.

After an hour's examination, during which he tested all my faulty coordinations, he would hand me a page of exercises and bid me take them twice a day. Then, with a little bow, his chin resting mournfully upon his paper tie, he would leave me to visit his next patient.

Sometimes — but only very occasionally — he would relax at the end of the lesson, empty his pockets of tobacco dust, roll himself a cigarette, smile, and take up his guitar and play to me for an hour. Then his eyes would turn inward and disappear into the echoing chambers of his mind, while his long white fingers moved over the strings with the soft delicacy of the blind, lost in a dream of melody and invention. And faced with the beauty of his technique, the complex harmonies, the ease and grace, the supreme mastery of tone and feeling, I would feel like one of the lesser apes who, shuffling on his knuckles through the sombre marshes, suddenly catches sight of homo sapiens, upright on a hill, his gold head raised to the sky.

Spanish bull-fighting is a thing of summer, of heat, dust and sharpest sun and shadow. Quite rightly it belongs to a time of hot light and hot blood, and one does not look for it in winter. Even so, there are occasional out-of-season corridas held for amateurs, for charity or as trial contests for promising boys. And such a one was held on our second Sunday in Seville, organized in honour of the Patron Saint of the Air Force, and we went to see it.

We arrived late to find the gates of the bull-ring locked and a large crowd struggling among a squad of mounted police. A man with a megaphone told them to go home, that the corrida had begun and the ring was full. We were just on the point of turning away when a party of gold-braided officers arrived, we fell in behind them, doors were thrown open, officials saluted us, and in no time at all we found ourselves ushered into a private box high above the arena.

Before us lay the classic scene: the ring of sand, the crescent of sunlight, the banked circle of spectators with dark-blue faces like flints in a wall, and the two almost motionless antagonists below us – the bull-fighter with bowed head, standing in silence; and coughing in the dust, a young bull dying.

We had arrived at the second kill of the afternoon ; but we saw four more, the best and the worst – the best magnificent, the worst a crime. In a corrida of this nature one may see anything. The young toreros, eager to establish names for themselves, are often capable of a feverish bravado, but more often suffer from a kind of hysteria which loses them control of both bull and themselves. The bulls, too, are often a green, unpredictable lot, capable of nobility, treachery and excruciating cowardice. Not rarely, in such circumstances, the boy gets killed as well as the bull.

The second bull that afternoon seemed to have been killed with some skill, for as the boy stood there with his blood-stained sword, he received no groans or hisses. A quartet of plumed horses dragged away the body, the sand was raked smooth, and we waited for the entry of the next. This is one of the great dramatic moments of every encounter ; the fighters take up their positions, the hushed crowd waits, then the huge doors to the bull-pit are thrown open and the unknown beast charges forth, fresh in anger, into the ring.

The trumpet for our third bull duly sounded, the doors were thrown open, the attendant scampered for safety, and we all waited ; but nothing happened at all. The attendant crept back and peered cautiously round the corner of the open doorway. He whistled and waved his cap. Then, gaining courage, he began to leap up and down in the mouth of the bull-pit, hooting and capering like a clown. Minutes passed, and still nothing happened. Slowly, at last, and sadly, lost as a young calf, the bull walked into the ring. He looked with bewilderment around him, turned back, found the doors shut and began to graze in the sand. If ever a body lacked a vocation for martyrdom, this sorry bull was it. He had no conception of what was expected of him, nor any inborn anger ; all he wished was to be back in the brown pastures under Medina and to have no part of this. And when it came to the point, he put up no fight at all and was killed at last without grace or honour, to the loud derision of the crowd.

Every corrida is run by a President, the formal figurehead who commands the various stages of the ritual, and his box stood next to ours. It was the centre of honour and dedication, to which each torero bowed at the beginning and end of his trial. And this afternoon it was decorated by the presence of four young girls all dressed in the handsome robes of fiesta. White lace mantillas clothed their heads, and over their shoulders they wore rich black shawls embroidered with scarlet flowers. They leaned their bare brown arms on the parapet, and chattered, and turned every so often to flash their teeth at the solemn gentlemen who stood sipping sherries behind them. Silly, self-conscious, but undeniably beautiful, they were not spectators but symbols, the virgins of the feast, flower-soft among the blood, providing that consrast of youth and death so beloved by every Spaniard.

A superb, straight-limbed young man now stepped forward
into the ring and a cheer went up, for he had already earned
some reputation. He was dressed, not in the heavy gold-
embroidered garments of the professional matador, but in Andalusian riding-clothes – a broad black hat, short waistcoat,
tight-fitting trousers and high-heeled boots. With cape folded,
hat held to his breast, he faced the President's box, bowed,
raised his head, and in ringing eloquent tones dedicated the
next bull to one of the virgins, whose name was Gloria. Her
companions congratulated her rather noisily upon the honour,
while she, huge-eyed and delicate as a doll, waved a small hand,
and then went pale as death.

The President leaned forward and gave the signal, the trumpet sounded, and the doors opened for the fourth bull. And this
time there was no doubt about it. He came in like thunder,
snorting and kicking up the dust, his black coat shining like a
seal's, his horned head lowered for immediate attack. Two as-
sistants, trailing long capes, ran out and played him first, a formal prologue designed to discover the unknown temper of the
bull, his way of charging, which horn he liked using, and so on.
Slowly, their job done, they were beaten back towards the barriers, and the bull stood alone. Then Gloria's champion walked
out across the sand. He took up his stand, the pale sun gilding
his rigid face, gave a loud clear shout to the bull, and from that
moment we witnessed an almost faultless combat. Elegant, firm-
footed as a dancer, but with cold courage and movements of
continual beauty, the boy entirely dominated the bull. He
seemed to turn the fury of the beast into a creative force which
he alone controlled, a thrusting weight of flesh and bone with
which he drew ritual patterns across the sand. The bull charged
and charged again, loud-nostrilled, sweating for death, and the
boy turned and teased him at will, reducing him at last to a
kind of enchanted helplessness, so that the bull stood hypno-
tized, unable to move, while the young man kissed his horns.
Alone in the ring, unarmed with the armed beast, he had proved

himself the stronger. He never ran, he scarcely moved his feet, but he turned his cape like liquid fire, and the bull, snorting with mysterious amazement, seemed to adore him against his will, brushing the cape as a bee does a poppy.

After the short barbed lances had been thrust into the bull's shoulders, drawing their threads of blood, the moment for the kill arrived; and this was accomplished with almost tragic simplicity and grace. The boy, sword in hand, faced the panting bull. They stood at close range, eyeing each other in silence. The bull lowered his head, and the crowd roared 'Now!' The boy raised the sword slowly to his eye, aiming horizontally along the blade; then he leaned far forward and plunged the weapon to the hilt in the bull's black heaving shoulders. Such a moment, the climax in the game, carries with it mortal danger for the matador. His undefended body, poised thus above the horns, is so vulnerable that a flick of the bull's head could disembowel him. It is the moment of truth, when only courage, skill and a kind of blind faith can preserve the fighter's life. But the boy's sword had found its mark, and the bull folded his legs, lay down for a moment as though resting at pasture, then slowly rolled over and died.

The crowd rose to its feet with one loud cry. Hats, caps, cushions, even raincoats, were thrown into the ring. The young man stood among these tributes and smiled palely at the crowd. Then he came, sword in hand, and bowed low to the President and to Gloria. Colour and intoxication had returned to the girl's cheeks; she stood up and clapped him wildly and threw him a box of cigars. His triumph was hers; it was the least she could do.

The rest of the afternoon was a sorry sight, an anti-climax. The fifth bull wouldn't fight, and just wandered miserably about the ring looking for a way out; he retreated when challenged, and leaned sickly against the barriers when wounded. The sixth and last was a fine animal, but he had a wretched opponent whom he treated with contempt. After a few hysterical passes, during which the new torero lost both his cape and his head, the bull turned irritably upon him, tossed him twenty feet across the ring, split his thigh and trampled on him. A volunteer took his place for the kill, bungled it, and was booed from the ring. Finally the bull was dispatched by an attendant's dagger.

Meanwhile the hero of the afternoon, who had been awarded two ears, was called to the President's box to meet the guests of honour. We saw him standing on one leg drinking sherry with Gloria, whose great eyes, running over his body, promised more dangers than any bull.

Our last nights in Seville now moved timeless, unsorted, gliding gently one into the other. I remember sitting in the Garden of Hercules at dusk, writing, sipping wine and being stroked on the nose by a whore. I remember walking the narrow crowded Sierpes, that serpent street of various temptations, listening to the hot voices of the youths undressing their fabulous and imaginary mistresses. Or exploring the dark, shut, oriental side-streets, where the locked-up girls gazed out at the world through heavily barred windows. The slow time dripped musically from fountains, wine-barrels and the guitarist's fingers. We moved through musky orange gardens, or down the Alamedas eating sweets, or watched the thick waters of the Guadalquivir brushing Triana's blue-glazed walls. These were nights turning towards Christmas, fresh, cold, with glittering pendulous stars.

A small boy stood in the doorway of a wine shop, thin, barefooted, with short and scruffy hair. The girl with him also had cropped hair, so that her head looked as though it were covered with scorched grass ; she was about eleven years old, but her dark slanting eyes were as quick and frisky as fish. The boy had come to sing. He screwed himself up and sang in a high passionate wail, throbbing, trembling, tearing his heart out. He seemed to be singing himself to death, as though each song was a paroxysm which diminished and bled his frail young body. And while he sang the girl perpetually watched him, anxious and maternal, echoing each phrase of his song with mute contortions of her lips. Afterwards she took him by the hand and led him round, charming us all for alms. But they preferred to be paid in monkey-nuts, which they could eat.

It was the time now when the streets were full of such children, when the ragged half-naked urchins from the hovels of Triana came out in force and filled the town with carols. In busy gangs they roamed about, carrying a host of home-made instruments – tambourines, castanets, drumskins, and tins which they scraped with sticks. At a word they would surround one and sing a whole concert for a penny. They were of all ages from four to fourteen, and they threw back their heads and sang with the ease and eagerness of angels, striking clear cool harmonies, and beating out the most subtle rhythms on their assorted instruments. Some blew into water-jars, making deep base notes; some rattled dried peas in boxes; others shook loose tin-lids threaded on a stick. I never tired of listening to them, for I had never heard or seen anything like them before. Their singing was as precise as though they had rehearsed for months, yet naturally spontaneous and barbaric, as though the tidings they brought were new, the joy still fresh.

The night before we left Seville I walked late in the streets alone. It was past midnight; men were repairing an empty road and there was a wet moon over the Cathedral. As I headed at last for home I ran suddenly into another of these gangs. They were sitting in an alley, warming their bare feet round a fire of burning paper. When I called to them they came crowding around me, squealing like starlings, grinning and arranging themselves in order. Their leader, a boy of ten, muttered a few instructions. Then they sang me five ecstatic carols, their smiles wiped away, their faces set in a kind of soft unconscious rapture. Here again, as in the others I had heard, was the same order, expertness and love. A girl of five took a solo, singing through the short tangles of her hair in a voice of such hoarse sweetness one felt shriven of all one's sins. As she sang, the others watched her with solemn eyes, their lips pursed ready for the chorus. In this shabby street, lit by the lamp above, their bronze heads seemed disembodied, like Botticelli spirits, floating and singing in the air. They sang of a star in the sky; of Christ and the Virgin; of Triana (across the river); and of Bethlehem (across the hill). And looking and listening to this ragged lot, I believed all their bright songs told me. For they lived near the heart of all these things, and knew what it was to sleep on straw in stables.

3. The City of the Sun - Ecija

We came to the city of the sun on the night of a full moon which rose like a tide over the azulejo towers and hollow rat-filled palaces. We had journeyed for five hours from Seville's December cold, but as we dropped down into Ecija the gusty winds went still, and the moonlight seemed to collect in warm pools along the little streets and to drip off the white walls with a visual texture as smooth and as tender as oil.

The centre of the city, antique and antic now with the social stir of the evening, greeted us with a glare and jostle that owed nothing to neon lights and motor-horns but was all of a natural piece, homespun and roughly local. It was the hour of paseo: boys to their girls called neat-turned adorations; loud cries from gritty throats celebrated the reunion of friends who had not seen each other for at least thirty minutes; lottery-ticket sellers chanted their chances of fortune; and a hoarse town-crier with drum and trumpet, announced a sale of mules. Around the square there were palm trees, white arches and blind secret windows; and it seemed as though the Moors had only left that morning.

It did not take us long to find our footing here. No sooner had we unloaded our bags upon the pavement, than six strong boys surrounded us, and with loud and eager civility promised to carry us to the lodgings of princes. They had tattered clothes, bare feet and the dark shapely faces of Arabs, they shouted and flashed their moonlit teeth and before we knew what was happening each had seized an article of luggage and all made off in different directions.

We were saved from this dilemma by a late arrival on the scene – a porter with a monstrous square head, sad eyes and a capacity for tempestuous rages. Screaming into the night, he called back every boy, stripped each of his load, piled it back on the pavement, checked it and then, with a miraculous arrangement of arms and legs, shouldered the lot and with a crooked smile staggered away before us to the Hotel Comercio, which he represented.

The Hotel Comercio was about as commercial as the cave of Ali Baba. Around the vast shadowy patio, shepherds, in fleece-lined coats, sat eating and drinking. Boot-blacks on their knees seized and polished the boots of anyone who stood for a moment near them. Two farmers were tasting each other's crop of olives and spitting them out with epithets of disgust. And a magnificent gypsy wandered among the throng selling silver Virgins and cures for love. The hotel office was a glass box, set like a fish-tank in the corner of the patio. Enclosed within its shining walls sat a handsome Sevillana to welcome us. She had heavily made-up eyes, a bursting poppy mouth, and hair like two gallons of coal tar. She left her crystal office and showed us to a bedroom full of white pillars, arches and fretted wooden panelling, for which, with food, we were asked to pay the price of one indifferent meal in a Knightsbridge café.

After a supper of squid and goat's flesh, we went out into the street and watched the moon flashing on the azulejo towers. They stood around in a rich mysterious company, brooding and glittering above the city roofs with ornate, unearthly presences. There were perhaps a dozen of them, all of a similar decayed magnificence, and every few minutes one or other shivered to the stroke of a bell which told one nothing dependable about the time but which filled the night air with a succession of soft feathery sounds as from magical beings who called to each other.

As we walked through the brilliant midnight streets birds on the warm walls sang as though it were day. And little beggar

girls came up out of the shadows and smiled at us and asked us
our names. Astride their hips each carried a sleeping babe, the
body of each was smoke-black under its rags, their dark curls
were caught in tangles which only scissors would ever unravel,
their feet were bare, their eyes diseased, but their smiles were
the roundest in the world.

With them we went to the booths under the arcades and
bought cakes, nuts and sunflower seeds. With them we sat round
the moon-twinkling fountain and ate a second supper. It was a
gay ravenous meal, and the sleeping infants were awakened
and forced to share it. Pieces of sugar cake were pressed to their
drowsy mouths; with eyes still closed they chewed and swal-
lowed, they groaned and gasped in half a dream, they were
coated with sleep like fur. But the young mothers, by shakes and
cries and kisses, made sure the little ones knew what they were
eating. It would have been improper otherwise.

The next morning was golden with inevitable sun, and Ecija
was at last revealed in all its decayed and gilded splendour.
Ecija is a small country town between Seville and Cordova. The
Romans called it Astigi, the 'city of the sun'; but Paco, the hotel
porter, calls it 'the frying pan of the world'. Lying in a depression among the hills it is like a lake of sun, a reservoir of heat.
It has a river, but never a breeze. In summer it is so hot that the
very natives fall dead in the streets. Even this morning, in mid-
December, the sun had the warmth of an English May, though
faintly water-cooled to give it freshness.

As we walked abroad again and looked about us the daylit
towers seemed to be stuck all over with wet violets, a moist
and effervescent blue as though they were still sweating from
the moonlight they had absorbed the night before. All round
the square, under the African palms, old men, wearing black
Cordobese hats, sat in stiff rows like figures at a judgement. Late
in their life though it may have been, these ancients still had a
sharp eye for a pretty woman. As Kati walked by, they looked

at her hard from under their hats. 'Behold!' said one, 'how like a ham she is.' 'Oh, for a knife and fork!' cried a second. 'Silence,' growled a third. 'Don't you see that she is a married woman?' 'Ah,' said the first with a sigh, 'but that she were a widow for only five hours.'

Soon the beggar children espied us again, and came running across the square, shouting our names and shaking out their verminous black locks. The infants hanging from their hips were now sleepily awake, peering around them with little red eyes. We all went down to the river-bank and sat by the water, and the children talked about their lives.

Isabela, the eldest, led the conversation, as she led in all things. She was about twelve years old, had a golden grimy face, and a manner of supreme and pretty confidence in the world.

'Our family is stupendous,' she said. 'There are ten of us and we live in one room. We have a table and chair and we cook in the street.' She began to giggle. 'We haven't a bed. We sleep on straw. And for this room we pay four shillings a month.'

She was not complaining so much as asking us to share in a joke. But one of the company, a boy with a diseased skin, considered she was boasting.

'I pay nothing for my house,' he said. 'It is mine.'

'It's not,' said Isabela, 'it's your mother's.'

'Well that's the same.'

'Anyway, it's not much of a house – all tins and palm leaves.'

'But it is ours,' said the boy.

The children all began to flow with information, competing with and contradicting each other. I asked them what their fathers did. They were all dead. 'Mine.' 'Mine, too.' 'And mine.' 'Yes, it is true. All dead.' They announced the fact with bright smiles, making gestures of sleeping with their hands. One had died of a cold, one of a fever, another apparently of eating beans. Two had been shot – *bang! bang!* – but I could not gather by whom. Yet I believed them, for Spain is a country of dead fathers, and today there are a million young widows in that country who will never see a second husband.

Another girl, up to her thighs in the river, was washing her brother's head. Her dark-brown face was tender and beautiful, and her thick hair, matted with dirt and straw, gave her the ageless look of a bronze sculpture.

'We sleep in a bed in our house,' she said. 'Three at the top and two at the bottom. And if we don't bring home ten reales every day we are beaten.'

Everybody squirmed with laughter at this. Filthy radiant faces were convulsed. It was obviously a private joke. Only the diseased boy looked solemn.

'Nobody beats me,' he said. 'I buy all my own clothes.'

At the mention of clothes, the girl in the river lifted her dirty coloured dress and began to catalogue the sources of her garments. Behold the torn dress, given; the short tattered vest, given; the canvas rag of shoes, bought from the mother of Carmencita, who died. 'They are good,' she said, 'and I wear nothing else.'

There, by the river, we spent the sunny morning. The thick green waters went slowly by, like summer grasses flowing in a breeze. The girls chattered. And the diseased boy lay back, and gazed up through the eucalyptus trees, and sang in a voice as gentle as a bird's, over and over again, this pretty song:

> *How beautiful is my truelove,*
> *How beautiful when she sleeps.*
> *She is like a red poppy*
> *Within the green wheat.*

Ecija at noon was a city of black and gold – gold of the roofs and towers in the sun, and black of the shadowed alleys and of the widows passing through them. A breathless provincial quiet hung over the tiny world, choking the young men as they walked like prisoners to the churches. Yet beneath all this, the stones and the flesh, the pagan world lay close. Enrique, the savage old barber in the square, could talk about Astigi as though it were just around the corner. Under the prim paths of the municipal gardens, he told me, lay an elaborate Roman pavement of gladiators, goddesses and leopards. In his youth an old Roman fountain still played in the city square, a thing of erotic beauty with four stone naiads whose naked breasts gushed water. 'Preciosa,' he said. 'More beautiful than the moon.' These naiads, though loved by all, were condemned at last by a bishop, and taken away and buried in the mountains. 'But you must see the mosaics in the Town Hall.' he said. 'Women and bulls. Gods and tigers. They also are preciosa.'

So we went to the Town Hall with him, and there on the floor of the Council Chamber (once a convent, and before that a Roman villa) lay a mosaic of most voluptuous refinement. Across the neck of a prancing bull reclined a superb Europa, and around them paraded bearded gods, carrying whips and branches of green leaves. There were also nymphs, flowers, animals and birds. The floor was dusty, so a porter came and emptied a bucket of water over it. The colours of the mosaics sprang instantly alive, the nymphs shivered, the flowers opened, Europa seemed to draw in breath and arch her peach-fed body, and the bull's rich flanks steamed darkly.

'Ay!' said the porter, gazing down. 'Behold that now. Some mornings I come in here, with my mind elsewhere, and I could swear a naked woman lies on the Council floor. I have wanted to cry out. It is like a miracle.' He sighed, and scratched himself under his smock, and departed, rattling his bucket against his thigh.

After luncheon we walked to the edge of the town to see the bull-ring. It stood in a circle of old white walls surrounded by tinkling goats. We knocked at a door in the wall and entered a small garden, where an old woman was cleaning a brass bedstead with sand. She had a red face like a paper lantern which crumpled when she smiled at us. 'Enter,' she said. 'Look about you, and I will send my sister.' We climbed some steps and pushed open a crumbling door and passed into the bull-ring. Big, empty, harsh and haunted, for two thousand years this saucer of stone and sand had been dedicated to one purpose, and even in this naked daylight it still exuded a sharp mystery of blood.

The little bent sister arrived to show us round. She had no hair, was courteous and sad, and talked of the greatness of other times. We walked across the silent arena, now overgrown with grass. She showed us where the bulls were herded before battle, eight stalls of stone with heavy doors which could be raised in safety from above. Here, once, came the greatest bulls of the Guadalquivir, and the greatest names fought them. All was decay and desertion now. The stalls were white with the droppings of birds; the door-pulleys were frayed and broken; a wrought-iron bull's-head over the entrance wore a flaking skin of rust.

'In summer,' said the old sister, 'when it is possible, and if the agriculture is right, and if the campesinos have money – then we hold a corrida.' Her hairless eyes blinked about her with anxious pride, and the bright sun shone on the broken seats, the weeds and the grass, and on the sagging doorway to the pits through which the huge black bulls once made their thundering entrances. 'You should have come thirty years ago,' she said. 'How precious it was.' She talked with a faint whispering sadness, her head on one side, half smiling, remembering and listening to the time; hearing again the dead crowds roar on those electric afternoons; sitting once more in her Easter dress, the round flesh back on her shrunken bones, her cheeks flushed from a dedication. She was the shrivelled spirit of the place. She fluttered her hands in sun and shadow. Here men and bulls had died before her eyes. And the flowers in summer were most beautiful to see. There, in that courtyard, they quartered the dead beasts – the best in Spain, the biggest and most barbarous. To that little room, she said, El Chico was carried, blood on his shirt, sweat on his long green face. In her comb and shawl she had run to the well, fetched water for him, and held his hand in his final panic. But he died. Those summers were all hot dust and glory. Would the agriculture ever be right again? Would the farmers ever return from the hills calling again for bulls? She shook her frail head and wondered and locked the great door and took us back to the little garden. There she gave us two sweet oranges from a tree, and wished us good-bye. She would not accept a tip.

On our last night in Ecija came a message from the telephone exchange to say that the Superintendent had killed a pig and that we must go and help to eat it. The Superintendent, an old friend now, was a lady of rare vitality who knew and could sing the whole of 'The Fair Maid of Perth'. She had six nieces to help her with the telephones, and the exchange was a merry place, much given to gossip, card-playing and long delays. We arrived to find the telephone lines choked, and a great feast of pork, butter-cakes and coñac spread out among the instruments. All the nieces were screechingly gay, except for the beautiful Lola, whose boy friend, a dentist, was late.

This boy was normally her greatest pride, for he was a youth of some versatility and could, it was claimed, speak English. This was true enough, in a way. But although his voice was perfectly normal when talking Spanish, he spoke English in a faint, high-pitched, tinny whine which was well-nigh indecipherable. This mystified me at first, until I discovered that he had learnt his English from an antique pre-1920 gramophone and could only be said to be suffering from too good an ear.

But this dentist was devoted to Lola, and spent most of the hours of courtship in his surgery gazing into her mouth. They thus enjoyed a unique, almost speechless intimacy. Yet tonight, when he arrived, Lola blazed with fire and fury and would have nothing to do with him. For a while he did card tricks, to try to curry favour, but no one took any notice. Meanwhile the aunt entertained by dancing, dressing up and singing down the telephones. But still Lola's great eyes glowered above the feast. The aunt wrung her hands in dismay and brought more pork, even photographs of her dead relations. Until the dentist, grown desperate at last, threw down his cards and produced from his pocket a plaster cast of Lola's teeth. 'Here you are,' he said, blushing angrily. 'I had meant to give it you for Christmas.' But all was now well. Everyone exclaimed with admiration, and Lola took his arm, laughing deep in her throat, and would not leave his side again for the rest of the evening.

Meanwhile, as the coñac warmed us, there was dancing in the patio, where the pig's corpse swung white in the moonlight. We danced till three; the nieces did the sevillana; the aunt recited 'The Siege of Saragossa'; the telephone lights twinkled unheeded; and we ate the whole side of the pig.

Next day we left in a horse and carriage, with pork chops in our hands. Paco, the hotel porter, gave us a parting present a poem specially and laboriously written in red chalk capitals on the back of our bill. It combined tributes to Kati's beauty with, somehow, a lament on the death of Manolete. Then we rattled away through the cobbled streets to the shouts of the beggar children.

At the outskirts of Ecija we paused, briefly, to look back at the city. It lay in its little pool of sunlight, eternally gilded, eternally drowned. The ghostly bells called dryly to each other, and the ornate towers rose high above the clay like the stumps of once exotic flowers left from some other summer.

4. The House of Peace - Granada

Granada is probably the most beautiful and haunting of all Spanish cities; an African paradise set under the Sierras like a rose preserved in snow. Here the art of the nomad Arab, bred in the raw heat of deserts, reached a cool and miraculous perfection. For here, on the scented hills above the green gorge of the Darro, he found at last those phantoms of desire long sought for in mirage and wilderness – snow, water, trees and nightingales. So on these slopes he carved his palaces, shaping them like tents on slender marble poles and hanging the ceilings with decorations like icicles and the walls with mosaics rich as Bokhara rugs. And here, among the closed courts of orange trees and fountains, steeped in the languors of poetry and intrigue, he achieved for a while a short sweet heaven before the austere swords of the Catholic Kings drove him back to Africa and to oblivion.

But Granada never recovered from this flight of the Moors, nor saw again such glory. When the cross-bearing Spaniards returned to their mountain city they found it transformed by alien graces and stained by a delicate voluptuousness which they could neither understand nor forgive. So they purged the contaminated inhabitants by massacre and persecution; and in the courts of the palaces they stabled their mules and horses. But the inheritors of Granada, even today, are not at home in the city; it is still dominated by the spirit of Islam. Fascinated and repelled by it, they cannot destroy it, but remain to inhabit an atmosphere which fills them with a kind of sad astonishment, a mixture of jealousy and pride. The people of Granada in fact, are known throughout Andalusia as a people apart, cursed with moods which reduce them at times to almost murderous melancholy.

Our first day in the city was lit by the dead white light of reflected snow, and after the soft-blown airs of Ecija, we were immediately chilled by it. The hotel was starched and fireless, so we walked out to warm our blood. We went across the Darro gorge and up the Alhambra hill, climbing a rain-torn path behind the Palace. Here, an oasis in the dry burnt south, were green trees, banks of ivy, flowers and gushing water. A bird sang a thin cold song, and the Palace glowed with a winter redness among its leaves. Climbing, and skirting the great wall, we came out on to a rocky cemetery road leading to the high place of the dead. Groups of mourners, laden with chrysanthemums, were going to the graves, and the road was strewn with gold and purple petals which exuded mournful odours under foot.

On the crest of the hill we sat down, with our backs to the cemetery wall, and looked out across the Vega. This was the highest point in the city, a favourite site for graves, and the view was tremendous. A thousand feet below us stretched the wide and populous plain, shafted with light and scattered with smoky villages. In the clear air one saw tiny figures, as though in a landscape by Breughel, scampering about in streets and squares. It was Christmas Eve, and a muttering air of holiday came up to us on bursts of the wind.

Across the plain, and huge to our northern eyes, stood the long range of the Sierra Nevadas, half-filling the whole sky. The foot-hills climbed in writhing terraces, great granite rocks threw shadows ten miles long, and the snow peaks, crisp as crystal, flashed among drifting clouds like a string of jagged moons.

In spite of its magnificent prospect the cemetery hill was not a popular place to live. Mourners and lovers walked darkly among the cacti and stunted olives. There was a solitary farm, high up; and here and there, though hidden among the rocks, a few brushwood hovels built by beggars. Otherwise the hill was left to the dead.

It was therefore rather surprising to see, on the edge of a cliff near by, a large brass bedstead with a woman and child lying on it. Pots and pans were scattered about the ground, but there was no sign of any habitation near. The woman lay silent, gazing at the sky, and the small child slept at her breast. Strange and surrealist it was, the naked bed, the child so still, the woman so unconscious of us. What could they be doing, exposed on the hilltop thus?

We were wondering about this, when suddenly, from the ground under our feet, appeared a boy with a basket of stones. He was about thirteen, very poor, barefooted, with dusty hair and a suit of clothes sewn together with string. He emptied the stones on the ground near by, and saluted us gravely.

'Where did you spring from?' I asked.

'Out of the ground,' he said, pointing downwards with a blackened thumb.

'That's what I thought,' I said. 'What are you doing? Gold-digging?'

'No gold there,' he said. 'Only stones. We are making a cave. Much work it is. Ay!'

'What is it for?' I asked.

He straightened his shoulders and lifted his head.

'It is our house. We shall live there. See my mother and sister on the bed? They are waiting to go in. Tonight all will be done. It will be a stupendous cave, tall, wide and will have a chimney. It will be the best cave in Granada.'

'Where did you live before?' I said.

'Down there, by the river,' he said. 'But a bad house, full of rain and frogs. Three sisters died coughing, and the landlord took all our furniture. But the cave shall be much better, dry, with a strong roof. When we move in we shall have a feast.'

While the boy was talking we heard a hoarse muted voice calling from under the ground. At first the boy took no notice.

Then we saw a man come out of a hole and crawl on his belly among the rocks. We also saw that the man had no legs.

'That is my father,' said the boy. 'He is very strong.'

He picked up his basket and left us, and it began to rain. The man and the boy crawled back into the ground, and immediately we heard the sound of the pick-axe under our feet. The woman on the bed lay waiting, making no sound. The rain fell on her face but she seemed not to notice it. The small child slept.

In a narrow street near the Cathedral we found a cheap café called 'The House of Peace'. And quite a find it was. For a shilling one could have soup, steak and chips, and fruit. A bottle of white wine, fetched from a near-by tavern, cost fourpence extra, and was as strong as a blow on the head. The company was mixed and noisy – mostly carters and thin hungry medical students – and in time we got to know it well.

The house was run by a large spreading family under the nominal head of one, Don Porfino, who was a melancholic and a drunk. He never did any work at all. But among the more active members of his staff were Trini, his beautiful tragic-faced wife, who did all the cooking; his old mother, who sat all day shivering among the potatoes; Elvira, a pretty quick-tongued widowed sister who served the food; and another sister, the fat, no-good Caridad, whose only value to the establishment lay in the fact that she had a butcher-lover who sold them bull-meat cheap. There were also two worn-down servant girls: Concha, a good-natured, sentimental dwarf; and La Sorda, a red-cheeked, short-sighted, half-deaf girl from the hills. These last two slept in cupboards behind the kitchen and spent their days in scrubbing the house, washing the dishes, peeling potatoes, running for wine, and fleeing from the embraces of the students.

On that afternoon of Christmas Eve, as we sat down for lunch in 'The House of Peace', the students and carters were in holiday mood and calling for second helpings. Elvira stood in the kitchen doorway, surveying them.

'You'll get no more,' she said. 'One plateful's enough, and one is all you'll have.'

'Go on,' they shouted. 'Even the cockroaches here eat better than we do.'

'You eat like kings,' she said.

'Ay,' muttered a carter, 'one meal here, and by five o'clock we're as empty as street-thieves.'

Elvira, keeping up a running battle with her tongue, wiped the grease from her hands and descended upon them. Weaving gracefully among the tables, she swept up their plates and drove them beaten into the street. When she brought us our steaks, she said: 'When you've finished, go and sleep, for you won't sleep much tonight.'

We asked her why.

'Tonight is Noche Buena,' she said. 'In Granada no one sleeps on such a night. All the world goes to the streets. There will be walking and singing all through the town, with pom-poms and bombas and radidas and bonfires – stupendous noise all night. You wait. You will be much diverted.'

She asked us if we had made any special arrangements, and we said no.

'Then you must eat with us,' she said. 'At nine o'clock we have a big feast here, with all the family at a long table. There will be wine and butter-cakes and all you can eat. The grandmother invites you, and so does Don Porfino.'

So we accepted gladly, and went out into the streets and found the shops making their last festive fling, with dolls of cut paper and rings of sugared cake for the children. Peasants were coming in from the country, driving flocks of turkeys before them, or carrying bunches of squawking fowls slung over their shoulders. In the market we bargained for a fat live cockerel and sent him back to the 'House of Peace' as a contribution to the feast.

But we did not sleep ; there was too much going on. Broody Granada seemed to be shaking out its feathers and gathering strength for a night of riot. People were hurrying from the market with wine in their pockets and carrying hens by the neck like umbrellas. By the cold coming of evening bright strings of braziers began to appear along the pavements, surrounded by squatting gypsies. With fiendish faces flickering over their fires, they were selling bombas and rattles to add to the noise of the night. The bombas were different to any others we had seen – earthenware pots, slashed bright with savage paint and sealed at the top with a drum-skin. The skin was pierced with an upright cane which gave forth hollow growls when you stroked it. The rattles were loose tins nailed to sticks, all richly coloured in reds and greens and purples. Such instruments, in the right hands, could fill the air with fine barbaric sounds, dark and devilish as any jungle. As night fell, we bought one of each, and walked through the rapidly crowding streets adding our lot to the din.

Granada, sealed among its mountains, began to stir and glow with a special enchantment, as though it were the only city in the world to rejoice at this time. It seemed to be caught in the throes of some local miracle, some imminent wonder to be revealed only here. It was Christmas Eve, but not like any other we had seen. The wintry air, both fresh and dry, was spiced with the wood-smoke of the fires in the streets. One smelt, too, a mixture of snow and desert, far off and strange. Fugitive fowls ran screeching under foot. All traffic stopped, and the Arab stars shone bright. And the marching crowds, with their bombas and rattles, moved through the roaring lanes in an atmosphere of primitive buffoonery and joy.

By seven o'clock one could scarcely move; one threaded one's way from bar to bar. Comic hats and false noses began to appear. We found a rich young man with two blonde girls, all wearing beards and black moustaches, and went with them on a spree. By this time I was merry, and playing a Moorish pipe.

Our whiskered friends, clashing cymbals, led us to a curious house full of hairdressers, dandies and dancing whores. Wine and dishes of sickly sweets were passed among us while a fat girl danced and stamped her feet till the combs fell out of her hair. The bearded dandies sat round her in a circle, clapping smartly and barking hoarse cries. The girl flared out her scarlet skirts and writhed her mouth and shook her shoulders, weaving among them roused and burning, her raw face hot from their eyes. She reached at last a sensual frenzy, a snarling smile on her face, throbbing, posturing and combing her body with her fingers, till her stamping feet filled the air with dust and she collapsed on the floor to the screeches of the hairdressers. One of these, a beautiful young man, then leapt on to an ironing-board and began to execute a fine-toed zapateado, flaring his nostrils and tossing his curls the while. Clearly the night's entertainment promised to be long and varied. But we had to go . . .

We arrived at the 'House of Peace' to find the feast already spread. Don Porfino's family, together with a picking of students and carters, had taken their places around the table and were drinking hard and snapping biscuits at each other.

'Behold!' cried the grandmother, her chin on the table, 'the sun and the moon have arrived.'

We were ushered, with pretty ceremony, to the head of the table, and immediately Concha and La Sorda began to bear in great platters of pork and rice. When, to the accompaniment of speeches, this had been satisfactorily dispatched, our cockerel, well roasted, was placed before us, and in spite of every protest, nobody else was allowed to touch it. There were thirty of us at the feast, and each of us, from the grandmother to the children, had his own bottle of wine, which was the colour of rain. Don Porfino sat on my right, and was already far gone with his drink. His face, like wet clay, was yellow and dead-looking and oozed with peculiar oils. His pale-green eyes crawled slowly over me, as though groping for support. His lips wore a sad and permanent grin, and his tongue fought stumblingly for words.

'Lorenzo,' he said. 'I am hot and sick. My head burns and my heart is dirty. Let us leave this shameful place. Let us go to the mountains and throw snow at each other.'

Trini, the wife, sat near, listening and watching with her tragic eyes. When she caught my glance she tapped her head and flicked an imaginary fly off her shoulder.

The hungry students, now bold with food, began to raise their voices. They threw mangled jokes at me, mangled compliments at Kati, which, having mangled further, we then threw back. The children screamed and covered each other with rice. The widowed Elvira looked young and shining and longing for love. And the little grandmother sank lower and lower in her chair, tearing her food with her fingers and squeaking like a mouse.

The feast grew noisy. We gorged and grew heavy, and La Sorda brought each of us a fresh bottle of wine. We began to sing ; and during the intervals there were exercises in wit in which even the silent Trini joined, revealing a sharp and flashing tongue, salty and edged with irony. But intoxicated as we all were, she stood apart, her black eyes ringed with pain, inhabiting a haunted territory of her own. I could not see what she was doing here. Her head on its long neck was proudly negroid, her brooding features ravaged and beautiful; she was straight and dark and savage, and she lived among that scheming, squabbling family like a hostage of royal blood.

We had pushed back our chairs now and were drinking coñac, and Don Porfino had wandered off into the cellars. The plump Caridad, her tongue well loosened, leaned across and began to tell me tales.

'My brother's a simple man,' she said, 'but kind, too kind. Look what he's done for her.' She jerked her head at Trini. 'Of course, she's not one of us. He found her in Morocco. And she is bad for him. Bad and proud. Though no one knows why, for she brought not a penny with her.'

I asked why she looked so ill.

'Oh, she has had a misfortune,' said Caridad, pulling a conventional face. 'Four days ago she was put to bed with a boy. He died, and she went out and threw him in the river. She is not strong yet.'

Don Porfino came back, singing a sad song, and dropped into his chair.

'Lorenzo,' he said, 'look at my face. Touch it. Feel my tears. I make myself weep. I have too much feeling.'

'Feeling!' spat Elvira, coming close. 'He has no more feeling than a sack. He is like all the others. Pigskins we women carry to the grave.' Her pretty face grew flushed and fierce. 'No, Lorenzo. The men of this country – pouff! – they are nothing. I pollute them all. Give me the foreign man, ay, there is the true gentleman.' And swift and hot she kissed me on the neck.

Meanwhile the students had advanced their chairs inch by inch across the room and were now sitting in front of Kati gazing upon her with glum desire. The first exhilaration of wine had left them, their eyes were glazed and their mouths hung open. They, too, had too much feeling.

At midnight we left the 'House of Peace' and went to the church to watch the Christmas Mass. The place was warm and scented and it seethed with a lively multitude. Walls and ceiling were starred with tiny lights, and the host of candles round the Virgin whirled, to my wine-struck eyes, like a cloud of fireflies.

Back in the streets, with midnight past, it was bright and brassy bedlam. The drums and cymbals crashed and thundered, and the wide pavements surged with young men, singing and fighting. It was the height of the night when anything might happen. Cries, salutations and groans of stifled desire greeted Kati as she passed. A tide of gallants began to follow her, lamenting her beauty and singing sad praises. One of their number, driven harder than the rest, detached himself from the group and approached her close, calling to heaven that he was helpless before such perfection. 'If I die for it!' he cried, and tried to embrace her. With drowsy dignity I took her from him and pushed him lightly away. But the crime was done. Outraged by his boldness, and shocked to silence, his friends leapt upon him, twisted his arms, and sat him on the pavement. Then they began to chatter and scold him, scandal in all their voices.

So we left them, and entered our hotel, which was near. We had not been in our room for more than a few minutes, when there came a loud banging on the door. It was Kati's victim, covered with shame.

'Go home,' I said.

'I cannot,' he answered.

He stood in the doorway, white, drawn and trembling.

'I have made a bad thing, sir,' he said, averting his eyes from Katl. 'I cannot go until you forgive me.'

'I forgive you,' I said. 'So go.'

He remained unmoving, his head downcast.

'My friends outside,' he said, 'they do not know you forgive me.'

'Tell them,' I said.

'No. You must show it, or they will never speak to me more. Go with me on your balcony, and shake my hand before them. Then they will know that my shame is forgotten.'

'Hell,' I said, and we went on to the balcony.

A solemn crowd of young men was gathered below us. In a frantic voice the boy began a speech of contrition, addressed to me and to all assembled.

'Behold,' he cried, 'the Frenchman has forgiven me! See, he is shaking my hand.' Here he pumped mine up and down. 'He is embracing me.' Here he threw his arms around me. 'We are friends.' Here he kissed. 'He has forgiven my offence. Viva el senor!'

'Viva!' roared the crowd.

I bowed; we both bowed. Then I dragged him off the balcony and pushed him out through the door.

'Good night,' I said, 'and don't come back.'

'Good night,' he said.

'Merry Christmas,' said Kati, ignored till then in these proceedings.

So we went to bed, but we got very little sleep. For the boy had grouped his friends beneath our window and organized a serenade in our honour, which continued, with songs, guitars and drums, till six o'clock in the morning.

Christmas morning; the streets empty, chastened and full of crumpled cymbals. So we went up into the Palace of the Alhambra, into the fresh gold air under the crimson roofs, to walk among the courts and fountains, to stroke the plump lemons and watch the fish. This was the first time we had been into the Palace, and one's immediate impression was surprise at its smallness. Here was none of the official bombast of Versailles and Blenheim, designed to impress by sheer weight of masonry. Instead a series of perfect little rooms, like tiny pavilions, draped themselves on slender pillars round courts of orange trees and water. Everything was open to the air, with fretted windows and pierced, arcaded walls framing green gardens and the distant hills. All was tender, feminine and intimately sensual. For the men who built the Alhambra were supreme miniaturists, scaling their work to set off a handsome, small-boned people, and preferring the epigram and the lyric poem to all forms of rhetoric and inflation.

It was a new dimension in architecture – or rather an old forgotten one. It grew like a flower on its many-levelled hill. The delicate pillars, reflected in the pools, shivered like the stalks of lilies ; the cloistered fountains trickled on leaves and lions ; and the small gold rooms gathered across their walls a quivering light of snow and water, asking only for a group of cloaked ambassadors or trousered girls to furnish them completely. This was the home of pastoral kings, of poet shepherds raised to glory, and looking upon its ornate surfaces one found no fault in it – only a profusion of exotic fancy controlled by absolute self-confidence and taste.

In the Palace gardens we ate a Christmas lunch of bread and raisins, and then, in the afternoon, followed a great crowd under a threatening sky to see another bull-fight. This was a special show designed to celebrate the first day of the Pascua. Six young Granadinos, nominated by their various supporters, had been voted into the ring to fight six young bulls as green in years and mixed in courage as they were.

We climbed to the wide concrete seats high above the arena and shared a cask of wine with a family from the Alpujarra. The bull-ring was crowded to the sky, the black clouds rolled down from the mountains, the air darkened, and the young toreros, in their tight suits, looked waxen and frightened.

The spectacle that now began was in many ways a repetition of the one we had seen in Seville. There was the same drawn intensity on the faces of the boys, the same brash courage alternating with bouts of hysterical panic, the same uneven, confused and often vicious bulls. It was their very youth that made them so dangerous. They came trotting in, their tasselled tails held high, cast puzzled eyes around the crowd, caught sight of some wavering challenge in the ring and charged or retreated according to their mettle. Then, with as much grace and style as the boy could muster, he would step forward and run the bull close to his body. Often, at this early stage, the bull's innocence made him charge the cape every time, and if the boy was lucky the passes were straight and clean, the bull's rushes shorter and tighter. This, like a successful dribble at football, was what the crowd had come to see, and its effect on them was like a shared orgasm, so that they shouted together 'Olé!' in one great voice, a loud excited noise to be heard all over the city.

It was in the later stages of the combat that the boys showed their inexperience, when the bull grew more difficult to handle, when the barbs of the bandilleros had torn his shoulders and he had grown angry and dismayed. Then he would stand alone in the middle of the ring, bellowing and dripping blood, or would wander miserably into a corner trying to escape. Only the best of bull-fighters could make anything of that situation, could lead the bull back into the fight and finish him cleanly. A less assured torero – like most of those we saw that afternoon – would run after the retreating bull with a kind of bitter sickness on his face, hating the whole thing; would wave his arms, and shout and caper, and sooner or later, in his frantic misery, get well tossed for his pains.

Everybody got tossed that afternoon, and some several times. There was one poor fellow named Angelito, a blond boy with large ears, who soon lost all control of his bull and was thrown round the ring like a shuttlecock. The crowd was much amused by this, especially our neighbour from the Alpujarra, who rolled in the aisles with delight.

'He is true to his name,' he said, when all was over. 'For he spends more time in the air than on the ground.'

This remark, I'm afraid, went well with the crowd, and was rewarded with wine from all sides.

But in spite of the occasional fiasco and the general hit, miss and run technique displayed by most of the boys, there was one young man who fought memorably. His name was Montenegro and he was sixteen years old, very thin, and had a face like a choirboy. He began badly, taking an early toss that split his trousers to the thigh. He rose from the dust, green in the face and trembling, and one thought his nerve had gone. But after tying a scarf around his leg, and stilling his quivering lips, he thrust out his chin and went on to fight like a little master. He took every risk, and yet he got away with them all. He ran the bull so close to his body that his shirt was stained with blood. When the bull grew sullen, and refused to charge, the boy turned his back on him and knelt down to show his contempt. He was brash, and showed off, and indulged in tricks which might have been thought vulgar, had he not, with each of them, invited his death. And in the end he killed his bull with such classical certainty that the crowd buried him in an avalanche of hats.

The afternoon ended with a diversion. The last bull had but freshly entered the ring, when an eleven-year-old boy leapt over the barrier brandishing a red-painted shirt. Attendants sprang upon him, but he dodged round their legs, fighting to get at the bull. A big man caught him and cuffed him and lifted him kicking from the ground.

'Bully!' roared the crowd. 'Put him down! Let him fight!'

With a twist of his body the boy broke loose, fell on his face, picked himself up, and ran straight at the bull. The bull charged him, and the boy, standing fetlock high, made two or three perfect passes, had his shirt torn to ribbons and was then trampled underfoot. But he was not hurt. The bull was drawn away and the boy was captured by a policeman. Then weeping with triumph, and to the cheers of the crowd, he was carried off to jail.

But the boy had made his name. In those brief stolen moments, alone with the bull, he had put up as good a show as anyone that afternoon, and better than most. And he had used the traditional method of calling attention to his courage – one which many a famous matador, in his young and starving days, had used before him. Moreover, he had fought in the bull-ring of Granada.

One glittering morning soon after Christmas we looked across the roofs of the city and saw the shining heights of the Albaicin and Sacromonte and decided to spend the day there. So we bought a flask of wine, some cheese and a bag of almonds, and set off up a cobbled lane which led in that direction.

The way was stony and steep, and climbed through an area of desolation we had never before visited. It was the cracked rim of the town, a crumbling cliff of decayed terraces smothered with mutilated cacti and stifled vines. Here were once the well-ordered gardens of the Caliphs, but the walls, now, were broken, and the sour earth spilled out among a scattering of tins and bottles. Shacks of beggars stood here and there and tents of black tarpaulin. Groups of young men sat silent in the mud, and the leaves of the cacti were slashed by their idle knives.

As we climbed the path that wound among these hovels, we saw a procession of black-dressed women toiling up behind us, carrying what seemed to be a doll in a long, flowered basket. They carried it lightly, and chattered among themselves as though returning from a day's marketing. But as they drew near and passed us, we looked into the basket and saw, peeping from among the flowers, the green dead face of a child. Four carried the basket, and a gossiping group of women followed. Then came some little girls with posies in their hands. And trailing behind, a whistling boy, with a coffin-lid under his arm.

We watched them thread their way among the cacti and disappear on to the open hill. No pomp, no priest, no men-folk at all. A child had been born, had died, and it was a matter for the women to take care of. So they would bury it on the hill, simply, like burying a bird.

But one does not brood on such things here. The climate is as ready with death as with birth. And in Granada, in the burnished, bright, but evil air, one is never surprised to find dead in the morning the friend with whom one walked and drank the previous night. It is this, perhaps, that makes friendship so intense here, conversation so rushed and hysterical, the company of the living so avidly sought. One can only be bored to death when there is a comfortable expectation of life. So we looked about us in the cruel sunlight, and ate some almonds, and went up the lane to the Albaicin.

In the time of the Moors this high place was set aside for the breeders of falcons, who kept their hooded birds in iron cages and trained them among the rocks of the hillside. From these steep slopes one can still peer down into the city with a falcon's eye or float one's gaze across the great spaces to the mountains. The houses of the falconers still stand, white and squat, their barred windows facing the Darro gorge.

It was here, in a cobbled square tilted steeply towards the sun, that we found a company of lace-makers, stitching and singing in the open air. A dozen girls sat round a table, their heads bent low over their needles, singing together in sharp high voices, and watched by a dark-faced woman. As we entered the square they called to us. 'We need some conversation,' they said. So chairs were brought, and wine and biscuits, and we were invited to rest.

The overseer, sharp-eyed but indulgent, warned us to take no notice of them. But no sooner had we sat down than we were assailed by a barrage of questions, jokes and speculations. The pretty creatures abandoned their work for a while and swarmed around us. They told us their names and exclaimed at Kati's beauty. They said I looked kind and strong and wore a handsome coat. Everyone talked at once, like birds biting cherries. They heaped us with lace and explained it proudly, showing us the needles, the stitches, the shapes and forms and speeds of their various skills. They made shawls, and wedding gowns, and veils for widows and the church. 'It is very difficult,' they said, 'but behold' – and everyone began to demonstrate, with swift brown fingers, how quickly a rose or leaf could grow from their agile needles.

There was one, however, who sat aside, crouching intently above her task, unable to do more than raise her head for a moment to smile at us. She was making a bridal veil for a countess, they said; she had been working on it for a month, and it must be ready in the morning. The gauze of lace was spread before her on a frame, and in the brightness of the sun her needle threaded through the foam like a flashing fish in a glittering sea. The long white veil, light as dust, was a mass of flowers and angels, most beautifully wrought. It would cost, they said, ten pounds.

We spent the morning among those girls, warm in their sheltered square. They took it in turns to work and entertain us. We drank our wine and struggled with their wit. In the background, children with bare bottoms rolled voluptuously on the sunny cobbles. A white pig was tied to the doorpost behind us. A knife-grinder, blowing his pipes, passed through the square, and a bearded tinker followed, wheeling a smoky stove. And the girls taught me proverbs, and Kati learned to embroider leaves.

The overseer stopped barking, and decided to call it a day. She fetched more wine and biscuits, and rolled me a cigarette. Soon there was clapping and dancing, and everyone stopped work. 'Watch La Mora,' they said. 'She is very flamenca and most diverting.' La Mora, a tall dark girl with Moorish looks and the cheek of a gypsy, came swaying across the cobbles, sweat on her lips and devilry in her eye. Posturing before us, and stamping her feet, she sang a song in a thick choked dialect, racy and ribald, with many verses.

Then came Carmencita, a beautiful vicious child of fifteen, and dragged me to my feet. 'Stand, man!' she cried, and danced around me with intuitive calculation in her eyes. She arched her body and brushed me with it, she twirled and snapped her fingers, her small face contorting with precocious sexual spasms. As she danced she whispered charms and sultry evocations. Afterwards she sat beside me, running her hands through my pockets and examining everything she found there with sly speculation.

The girls loved Kati as though she were a doll, stroking her hair and exclaiming with pleasurable amazement if she said anything at all. And the overseer, having produced a rich black veil and gazed at it for a long time, suddenly made up her mind and pressed it upon her as a gift.

'Come back,' they said, when we were ready to leave. 'Come back at five o'clock, and we will make a paseo, and go up the hill to see the waterfall.'

So we said we would, and left them, and went up among the cactus groves to the caves of Sacromonte. This was gypsy country, where tourists are fair game, and although it was the close season we had not long to wait. There was a panting and giggling behind us on the path, and two bright-coloured, grease-haired girls appeared, plucking our coat-sleeves and pleading famine. One of them carried a fat brown child across her hip, and she held him up for us to see.

'Have pity on this poor one,' she said, dropping her rich voice to a whine. 'Look, he is crying with hunger.'

He was not crying at all, in fact; he was grinning up at the sky like a plump young pasha. So the girl pinched him slyly, and he threw back his head and bawled:

'Hark now,' she said. 'He is dying of hunger. How can you see such suffering?'

Fair was fair, so I gave her a coin. Immediately she smothered the child with kisses, and with a swirl of scarlet skirts ran screeching down the hill.

The caves among the cacti were throbbing with guitars. Dark men, dressed like modern American Indians in tall hats, black suits and blankets, sat smoking and gazing at the Sierras. Huge black pigs ran squealing out of the caves, and bangled women walked stiffly by. Through their long sharp eyes the men watched us as we passed. If they had thought it worth while they would have whistled up their women and made them dance forthwith. But no. We had no cameras and were obviously without money, so they let us go by. Yet farther down the hillside, bright as butterflies against the tawny soil, a group of girls were dancing for its own sake, twirling among the cacti with a kind of intent and secret pleasure while their men sat round them on the rocks clapping and crying softly.

Gypsies are one of the aristocracies of Spain: indolent, insolent, rapacious and admired. They have annexed for themselves the folklore of the country, which they exploit with a brilliant and swashbuckling technique. Also, vulgar as their approach may be, they are able to maintain it with a vitality which the exhausted working peasant is not always able to provide. It is therefore through the gypsy that the Spanish tradition — suffering little competition from foreign film or radio — has been preserved at a high pitch of excitement in forms that only the gypsy himself can corrupt. The gypsy remains both traditionalist and innovator, bringing the fire of a professional vocation to his art and using music and the dance as charms to ensnare the gringos. Thus he has become a special caste in Spain, and the centre of that caste lies here among the caves of Granada. It is from these gaudy, whitewashed holes in the hillside of Sacromonte that many of the greatest singers, dancers and guitarists have sprung. Indeed such an aura still hangs about the place that almost every Spanish artist, at one time or another, will claim to have been born here.

We left the caves and climbed to the hill-top and lay at last under a Moorish wall and drank our wine in the sunny wind. From far below came the crying ejaculations of the dancers, the sounds of singing and squabbling, the steady throb of guitars. Among the explosive blue swords of the cacti the men sat black as coal, and the prancing women, their bright skirts opening to the wind, fluttered like blown geraniums. They were a circus at winter quarters, twirling, twisting, inventing, scheming, unable to keep still for a moment, limbering up for the coming of spring.

Up here, under the fortress wall, we were alone, save for a boy who was catching birds. He had set two caged sparrows on the grass and surrounded them with traps of lime. The birds sang sweetly, luring the wild ones to their doom. The deep gorge of the Darro lay black in shadow, and sun-slashed terraces rose up to a crest of trees where the slender Alhambra rode on green waves like a ship of fantasy. The sun shone through its upper chambers, giving them the lightness of air ; and behind, far off, but sharp as cut paper, the brilliant ranges of the Sierra hung naked in falls of new crisp snow. We finished our wine and stretched in the dreamy heat. From across the valley came the echoes of pedlars, donkeys and slumberous bells, and up from the city the continual sound, like drumming rain, of footsteps, voices, cockerels and horns.

To this, and to the whistle of the caged birds, we fell asleep ; and awoke much later to a new pattern of shadows and an edge of cold. It was five o'clock, and we went down the hill to the lacemakers, who were expecting us. All was ready for the even- ing paseo. The girls had rolled up their laces, changed their dresses, and hung their ears with flowers. We formed up in procession, dogs barked, pigs squealed, and heads were poked out of windows to wish us good-bye.

Then we set off, about twenty strong, with a wine jar and skipping-rope to visit the waterfall. Up the road we went in convoy, with naked children diving and rolling under our feet like dolphins. There was Carmencita, Isabelita, Antonita, Teresa, Rosario, Consuelo, Asención, Caridad, María and Incarnación. Some linked arms, some danced in the road, some skipped with the rope, all sand; and I, the only man among them, felt quite eleven feet tall.

It was a fine evening and everybody was out of doors. As we marched, so our numbers grew; we gathered girls like burrs and boys like fleas. We were soon a small army and the road was choked with us. The wine jar passed from hand to hand, and when it was empty a small boy darted off and filled it up again at a tavern. La Mora was in the highest spirits. In her foghorn voice she shouted to everyone she saw, 'We are going to the waterfall!' and, when they said 'What?' she said, 'To the waterfall, look!' and drenched herself with wine.

Half-way up the hill, high above Granada, we paused on a bank to rest. By now we were a minor multitude and were at- tended by a group of itinerant merchants – garbanzo sellers, peanut vendors, chestnut roasters and fortune-tellers – who followed us closely and kept us well supplied. As we sat on the bank above the road I sent for six more litres of wine and we drank it at one go. Its effect on the girls was lyrical and sad. In their haunting harmonies they sang of terrible deeds of love, of hearts' blood let by jealous knives and bleached bones in the snow. The excited boys, attempting to join us, fought and scrambled and rolled down the bank like pebbles. La Mora, flushed and sweating, led the singing in a high passionate wail. And sharp and sweet in the sweet-sharp air the songs of the girls led us on through ballads of blood and languor, while Carmencita wriggled close against me and stroked my arm, shameless and husky, praising my strength and asking for presents.

At this point an old gentleman in a frock-coat appeared from behind some bushes and took a photograph of us all and developed it in a bucket. On its curled black paper it looked like an ancient rock-drawing, all stricken postures and staring animal eyes. With this in our hands we went on up the hill and reached the crest of rock where the waterfall burst forth. In the green rush of roaring water the girls splashed themselves and floated leaves and sticks. Then the sun went down on the Sierra Almijarra and we turned at last for home.

A cloud of vermilion dust hung in the sky, while the earth grew blue and dark, a vivid shadow racing across the plains. Stamping and singing, the girls marched down the hill, while the young boys followed at a speechless distance. The snow-peaks changed from rose to ashen grey and the city pricked up its lights. Our progress was a triumph, a snowball of noise and clatter, gathering in strength to over a hundred strong, while the boys turned somersaults in the road before us, and fought and threw stones at each other, and everybody sang, and we entered the town in glory.

Back at last in the little square of the lacemakers, with darkness on us, we stood and collected ourselves. Fathers came out from the lighted doorways and rolled me cigarettes. Mothers gathered around Kati and praised her beauty and told her how long the Spanish nights were and how easy it was to beget children, so long they were. And the unmarried girls stood listening in the lamplight, their faces clear and knowing.

Finally there were games in the shadows, games in a ring, games of invitation, of pursuit and capture, dancing on the cobbles, chanted songs, and then good night. 'Good night,' they cried, from their doors and windows, and down the hill we went, through the squatting gypsies, out of the suburb and into the city.

The 2nd of January was the anniversary of the liberation of Granada by the Catholic Kings. It was, of course, a holiday, and the crowds took early to the streets. We followed them first to the Cathedral, to gaze upon the marble tombs of Ferdinand and Isabella – extravaganzas of sugar-icing most cold and rhetorical. In the courtyard of the Cathedral a troupe of horsemen were sitting at ease, scratching and arguing and waiting for the procession to begin. They were dressed in the traditional sixteenth-century costume, ill-fitting and much worn, and their dusty periwigged heads were topped by slack-plumed three-cornered hats. The horses were much worn too, weak-kneed and drowsy, saved from the knackers for the day, pathetic creatures all. Inside the Cathedral a splendid parade of priests, bishops, choirs, soldiers and city fathers moved to the high altar to begin the Mass. The place was full; the singing poor. The Archbishop sat slumped on his throne, reading a gilded book and extending his hand to the lips of the priests. A starveling monk, with a voice of sonorous gloom, began a sermon: 'My Lord Archbishop; Your Excellency the Governor of Seville; Your Excellency the Governor of Granada; Your Excellency the Military Governor of our fair Province; Holy Fathers and Brothers in God : now is the time, as never before, to be strong in Faith like the Catholic Kings ...'

But it was deadly cold in the cathedral, cold with damp words and stone, so we abandoned the Mass and went out into the weak sun and made our way to the Town Hall where crowds were already gathered. At twelve o'clock a posse of mounted police came jogging down the street, dredging a pathway through the multitude. At last came the sound of music, and the seedy horsemen appeared, leading the procession from the Cathedral. There were brass bands, state police, Civil Guards and some regiments of stern soldiery in German-style tin hats. They deployed on the great square and formed up in ragged ranks. Then came the black limousines of the dignitaries, full of tubby generals, bishops and governors, who entered the Town Hall to a rattling presentation of arms. The crowds pressed close around the square, and we waited. Presently, to the sound of bells, a handsome young officer stepped on to the balcony and raised a standard above our heads. The city went as still as an armistice silence; then the officer lifted his face to the sky and roared 'Granada!' in a voice of power. He called the name three times, and each time the crowd replied with the one word 'Que?', each time growing in strength, till the third response seemed to cover the city with a many-tiered, drawn-out cry with the children's screams on top. There was a pause, then the young man took a deep breath, raised the standard high, and called in ringing tones:

'In the name of Don Fernando the Fifth of Aragón, and of Doña Isabella the First of Castile: Viva España!'

'Viva!' roared the crowd.

'Viva Franco!'

'Viva!'

'Viva Granada!!!'

'VIVA!!!'

At that the piece was said, the cry of liberation recounted; the brass bands played some fascist hymn, the great ones went to a banquet, and the crowds dispersed. But they did not go home; all day they packed the streets, threading up and down like shoals of fishes, nibbling at each other's company.

So that afternoon I climbed out of the crowded city and went up the Alhambra Hill to look again at the Sierras. For several hours, on a crest of stones above the cemetery, I lay inert, breathing the thin deceptive sunlight and gazing at the pure and

spacious snows, unable to leave their sight. Over the plain lay a
chill blue mist – a still air coated with cold – and the wood-
smoke of the distant villages climbed out of it in sunlit tendrils
white as wool. Inside the cemetery walls, among the cold chaste
marble statues, forty dark graves lay freshly dug, waiting the
winter crop of dead. They would not have long to wait either,
so I was told, for Granada's winter air is a killer, moving so slow
it will slay a man yet not seem strong enough to blow out a
candle.

I lay looking down at the graves and felt cold in my bones ;
and yet I could not leave. The day was quiet and golden among
the hills, and a kind of terrible acquiescence held me in thrall.
A boy and a girl from the caves climbed up to beg. The boy
came first, while the girl stood at a little distance, framed against
the snow, watching his performance. He began briskly, confi-
dently, then his voice tailed away into a series of mumbling
entreaties, while I lay paralysed, unable to move or answer him.
Suddenly he broke off altogether, a look of fear came into his
face, and he turned and fled. Rejoining the girl, they both stood
watching me in silence for a moment. Then the girl started to
taunt and upbraid him, until, with a quick burst of anger, he
seized her and pushed her towards me. She came uncertainly,
pausing every so often to look back over her shoulder at the
boy, until he began to throw stones at her, driving her on. At
last she stood looking down at me, a round-eyed mask pinned
against the sky.

'We are hungry,' she moaned. 'We have no money to buy
bread. My mother weeps.'

With great effort I reached a peseta into her hand and she
gave a short laugh and flew off down the hill, the boy at her heels.

Through the long afternoon I lay there, while the sun moved
over half the sky and began to fall away. It was a cold, lost,
brilliant world, inhabited by solitary shades. I saw a man standing on the edge of a cliff, his back to the light, making water in
a shining arc of silver that fell away into the valley. Another,

who had been gathering grass, returned to the caves singing a flamenco which fell frail and naked on the ear. Among the tombs the mourners stood like cypresses.

As the sun sank, the bright paper landscape crumpled and contorted with savage shadows. The bare furrowed foothills of the Sierras writhed and dimpled like brains. And the snows, from the vivid incandescence of daylight, turned pink, mauve, purple, cold as slate, like the face of a dying man slowly drained of his blood.

I walked back shivering through the dusky olive trees, where a pair of lovers clung together under the dark boughs, the man silent, the woman lamenting in a trance-like voice some coming separation.

The next day I was taken with a fever and I went to bed. We had now moved our quarters to the 'House of Peace', at the invitation of Don Porfino.

'Lorenzo,' he had said, 'you spend your money like a torero. Thirty-five pesetas for that hotel room and not a lick of food. What d'you do it for? Come to us and for a miserable fifteen pesetas you can live like kings, with food, wine, good beds and a warm kitchen to sit in.'

So when my fever started I found myself in this clean whitewashed room overlooking the Calle Alhondhiga, and I was glad enough to be there. Slowly the fever took possession of me, and all day I lay shaking and cursing, my head full of sliding fancies, while Kati sat sewing in the window and the family came and went with various brands of comfort. First, Don Porfino, with a pint of coñac wrapped in newspaper; next, the brusque Trini, with a glass of hot goat's milk; next the dwarf Concha, who stood on tiptoe and gazed at me in silence, then shook her head and sighed and stole away. La Sorda, when she came, was hearty, and bid me rise like a man and not lie lazy there. But when the grandmother tottered in she gave me one look, and then settled down as though ready to make a day of it, folding

her thin hands in an attitude of waiting, and mumbling to herself a long story about the death of her husband. When at last
she took her departure, she spoke no word to me but touched
Kati on the cheek and bid her be strong. Apart from the coñac
and the goat's milk I got little comfort from any of this.

By the evening I was worse, and news of my condition had
reached the restaurant downstairs. After dinner about twenty
medical students came crowding into my room. First they saluted Kati with twitching moustaches and rolling eyes, then they
gathered round my bed and looked me over with speculation.
They began to suggest obscure medieval remedies, cupping
and blood-letting, all of which I declined. There was much shaking of heads and windy sighing, but when they saw that I was
abandoned to my fate their spirits brightened, they began to
puff out their lips and steal sidelong glances at Kati, like goats
on the brink of some luscious pasture, wondering which way
to jump. 'At least you must eat, señora, they said. And feeling
that they had done their duty, they bore her away downstairs.

Then I grew delirious and lost all sense of time. I was dimly
aware of nights and days, of the faces of Trini and the grandmother coming and going, of Kati sitting motionless in the window, and of crafty students peering stealthily in. But chiefly I
was aware of chill Granada, of the forty graves lying open on
the hill, of the fatal air that would not blow out a candle, and of
the gigantic, smothering visions which raked and consumed me.
I remember waking in the dark of the night, my knotted limbs
ice-cold, to hear the screech of a bird hovering with frost-white
wings over the silent town. I remember hearing the tramp of
feet one morning as they bore away a corpse from the house
next door. I felt doomed, resigned and full of mortal infection.
I felt I would never escape Granada's damp embrace. I would
die and lie out on the beggars' hill, under the stones and the
snow, but one more northern victim of this treacherous southern air. I mourned for the beech roots and willows of a Cotswold graveyard, for the casual cuckoos and climbing briars and

the sounds of cricket over the wall. I began to talk to myself, wryly, monotonously. 'Sperms – germs – worms,' I said, over and over again, yielding up my life to the three-word poem my fever had invented. There followed days of boiling blood, groans and demented images, when sleeping and waking merged into each other and became indistinguishable, furnished alike by faces, voices, melting bones, screeching birds and burning ice.

Then I remember waking one evening to a more normal consciousness to find the grandmother holding my hand, her creased, dried-walnut face rocking gently over me. A guitar played softly in a distant room, sad and cool, like dripping water. The town seemed unusually silent.

'Do not worry yourself, Lorenzo,' said the old woman. 'Resign yourself to the Holy Mother and make your peace. Whatever happens we will look after Kati. She is a good girl and works well and all the world loves her. She shall stay with us and be our daughter. Do not worry about her.'

She blessed me and left me, saying that Don Porfino would make all the arrangements. Presently came the jaunty Sorda, who squinted brightly upon me.

'Ay, Lorenzo,' she said. 'How lucky you are. Everybody is saying what a beautiful widow the señora will make. Even now the students make speeches to her. She will never want for a husband. Do not concern yourself about her.'

Unmoved, I fell asleep, but when I woke again, much later, it was to find Kati sitting by my bed, most calm and silent, dressed all in sombre black. She sat stiffly, in the waiting posture of the grandmother; her hands were folded in resignation, and her great eyes said Farewell. It was night, and very quiet, and yet I seemed to hear, from outside the door, the low whispering of the students patiently waiting also.

A sudden rage consumed me. I sat bolt upright like Lazarus in his sheets.

'Take that stuff off!' I cried. 'And clear those bastards off the stairs!' Kati jumped to her feet as though a ghost had spoken.

There was a moment's silence; then I heard the stumbling of the suitors as they stampeded into the street.

From then on I improved rapidly. I no longer heard the night-bird screeching over the town. The sounds from the streets were healthy; and the trotting of donkeys, tinkling of bells, the motor-horns, cockerels and stirring of distant trains all suggested a likely tomorrow.

Each day I read books with more interest and grumbled more vigorously. From the kitchen I was constantly supplied with hot-water bottles, hot milk, hot lemon, coffee and coñac. Two of the senior students, half doctors that they were, seeing me mend, fought one last rearguard action. They came with black bags and hypodermic needles and prepared a nameless injection; but I drove them from the room. After that the fact of my survival was accepted by everyone, all was forgiven, and the students brought me presents and even entertained me with card-playing and dominoes.

When at last I left my bed I spent my convalescence in the kitchen with the women. Here it was warm among the banks of stoves, and I was restored by roasted steaks and generous draughts of wine. Each morning the servants and the grand-mother peeled several hundredweights of potatoes while Kati fried them for the famished students. For the rest we sat round a brazier of glowing charcoal and sipped liqueurs, and talked. The conversation of the women was curiously inflammable, often obscene, flaring up sometimes into screaming rows which changed as quickly into squawks of laughter. They discussed love, murder, the price of meat, the fatness of Franco and the parts of their men. If ever I tried to say anything, the grand-mother would hush her daughters imperiously. 'You must listen to Lorenzo,' she would say politely. 'He knows life with his bones.' But how they knew it, those women, illiterate as they were, croaking together over their stoves like a chorus of wit-ches reviewing the turning world.

So passed our days in that rank warm kitchen, while the

great pans hissed on the stove, and Trini and Kati stood side by side, shaking and prodding the spitting meat. Armies of cockroaches marched over the walls. Sacks of potatoes were peeled and eaten. Bottles were drunk, and histories told. It was the women's world, and men had no part in it unless they wanted something – food, or warmth, or money. Sometimes Trini's three sons would appear, but fleetingly, for they lived at the clubs. Enrique, the youngest, was a mathematical genius and scorned all women. Manolo, the next, was a neurotic, given to sudden shaking rages, and was denied nothing. But Juan, the handsome eldest, was the pride of all, though he spoke little to any of them. He had seduced La Sorda when she first came to the house, but now he took no interest in her. When he came for his meals she would raise her head for a moment and watch him with her short-sighted eyes, then shrug her shoulders and return to her work.

But Don Porfino, the moody melancholic patron, had disappeared altogether from the scene. His wet, wine-sodden face no longer appeared in the mornings to wish me a grizzly day. For three weeks he had shut himself up in his room, with drawn blinds, cut off from life and from the light of the sun. No one could tell me why; and he never appeared again. Later, back in England, we heard by letter that he had remained for six months shut up in that room, drinking, reading comics, but never stirring. Then, one morning, he had cut his throat with a razor.

The day before we left Granada I at last succeeded in meeting the great Don José B., once a friend of the poet Lorca, and now one of the rulers of the city. The meeting was arranged by a poor journalist named 'Horsehead' who fed at the 'House of Peace' and worked as a hack for the Falangists. The negotiations had taken a month to complete, and Horsehead had treated the whole affair as a major conspiracy, planning each move with bated breath, for he was frightened and nervous, and Don José was a powerful man, and Lorca a tricky subject. However, in the end he fixed it, and came to my room with trembling limbs to announce that owing to his influence, and because of my esteemed interest in literature, the great man would see me.

I was taken that night to an opulent club near the Puerta Real and shown into a private room. Don José, a tall, grey, handsome man in his late fifties, greeted me with courtesy and warmth. He enquired after my fever, ordered coñac and biscuits, and invited me to sit with him at a wide window overlooking the moonlit mountains. There, in his rich classical Spanish, he talked at some length about literature and music and the gardens of the Generalife. The forbidden subject hung fire. Meanwhile, Horsehead sat at a respectable distance away, his hat perched on his knee, watching us with agonized eyes and twisting his nervous hands. Don José talked on and on, and seemed to grow more and more embarrassed. At last I gave him an opening, and he seized it gladly, and his face grew tender and haunted.

'Ah, Federico!' he said, in a changed voice. 'There was a man! – an angel of the arts, a veritable torrent of inspiration. He was a treasury of talent – writing, drawing, singing, playing the piano, everything he did captured the imagination of us all and transformed our souls. He talked like a god, and when he sang the gypsies were dumb, they sat transfixed and wept real tears. He was a spirit. He lived like a star. He seemed on fire. I was the companion of his youth, and night after night we walked by the river and he talking till dawn. He had three imperatives for poetry: "Luz, alma y vida"; and he loved Spain with his bones. Those wonderful records he made with Argentinita, he playing the piano and she singing his words! – to hear them now is to be scalded with fire and grief. He was all beauty and genius, was Federico. But he did not belong to this world. He travelled to America and made a lot of money, but the success shamed him. When he came back he said to me, "José," he said, "once upon a time I had no money, but my pockets were stuffed with poems. Now my pockets are stuffed with dollars, but I have no poems any more." '

As he was talking we were joined by two other friends of Lorca, both successful writers, and one the brother of a leading Spanish poet. Don José led them into the conversation, and how sentimental they grew, how they praised 'Federico's' memory and how they protested their love. They sang me his verses and wrote out in my notebook some of the words of his fandanguillos. Even Horsehead joined in, and for a time we seemed at ease. But when suddenly I mentioned his death, how swiftly their attitudes changed. What evasions, excuses and tortuous explanations followed. They all talked at once, pulling up their chairs, tapping me on the knee, and blowing their hot breath in my face. It was an accident, it was a private murder, it was a case of mistaken identity, it was a blunder by a Civil Guard who has since been punished – every story was different, except in its effort to prove that the killing had not been political.

But in the first hysteria of the Civil War, when some cities stood for, and some against, the rebel Franco, it was those with the guns who did the killing. And it seems that Lorca, in Franco-held Granada, was a marked man from the very beginning. For he wrote verses to traditional tunes which anyone could sing. They were sung widely, particularly by the poor, who do most of the singing in Spain. They were even sung by the anti-Franco armies. So Lorca was considered to be a red poet. He had also written several popular poems attacking the brutal Civil Guard. Many a man was shot for less cause in those first days. So Lorca was taken out on to the hills one morning and shot too. Excuses remain, and reasons are vague, but the poet is dead, and the guilt is Granada's.

5. Castillo of the Sugar Canes

We had come down now to the warm south coast, to a small fishing village which I shall call Castillo – though this is not its name. Many years ago, in the summer of 1936, I had lived in this place. I was there when General Franco made his journey from Morocco and the Civil War exploded along the coast. I saw this poverty-stricken Castillo lift its head out of the smoke and clamour of those days and feed, for a brief hour, on sharp hot fantasies of a better world. I had come back now, as I knew I must one day, to see what the years had done to the town. I found it starved and humiliated, the glory gone, and the workers of the sugar fields and the sea hopeless and silent.

Castillo was once a pirate stronghold, standing on a fortress rock in the mouth of an estuary, surrounded by water and hooded by mountains. The estuary, now, was dry; the castle ruined and stuffed with graves; and the town, stripped of its pirates and Barbary jewels, depressed and desolate. The silted estuary now grew crops of sugar cane, and the ragged shore was littered with broken boats. The fishing was niggardly, and the sugar offered little more than a month's work a year. For the rest of the time the townsfolk scavenged among the rocks or sat watching the sea and praying for miraculous shoals.

We put up at the white, square, crumbling hotel where, during my earlier visit, I had worked as porter and minstrel. The hotel was empty now and a wind of chill ghosts blew through the passages. We were offered our choice of rooms and took the best one, which had a balcony overhanging the sea. Below the windows a group of exhausted fishermen lay face downwards on the sand, sprawled out like starfish sleeping. Behind the hotel the promenade of cheap cafés, which once hummed with the talk of a world republic, now gaped at the sea with the empty eyes of beggars. The fountain was choked with refuse, goats browsed in the ornamental gardens, the sugar canes rattled like bones on the wind, and the dark-blue mountains stood close around, sharp and jagged, like a cordon of police.

A silence as of sickness hung over the place now, and I re-membered Castillo as I had seen it long ago. A summer of rage and optimism, of murder and lofty hopes, when the hill-peasants and the fishermen, heirs to generations of anonymous submis-sion, had suddenly found guns in their hands and unimaginable aspirations in their breasts. I saw them shoot the fish merchants, drive the sugar planters into the hills, barricade the mountain roads, and set up the flag of their commune over the Town Hall. 'This flag,' they said, 'will be defended to the last drop of our blood.' And so, indeed, it was. The smoke of violence and excess filled the streets in those first days. They looted the food shops, tore down the sugar factory, wrecked and burnt the Cas-ino. I saw a grand piano, like a monstrous symbol, blazing one morning outside the church. As it burned, the tense wires inside it snapped and jangled, while the keys, like teeth, spilled broken onto the cobbles.

The destructive frenzy soon wore itself out. The committee of the commune took over all the big houses that had been aban-doned by their owners, and across the walls, in letters of scarlet, they chalked their naïve ambitions. 'In this house we shall make a school for the women.' 'Here shall be founded a club for the young.' 'This house is reserved as a hospital of rest.' 'This house shall be the orphanage.' The committee sat night and day in the Town Hall, their guns on the table, confident that their enemies would be defeated; in the meantime drawing up an impossible, spring-like way of life.

Their plans were swiftly doomed. Very soon the yellow snub-nosed tanks came clanking along the road from Málaga, Italian bombers swooped over the Sierras, German warships shelled from the sea. The town fell; and the firing squads cut short the brave words of the committee; the big houses were restored to their owners, the writing was scrubbed off the walls; and Castillo's summer dream was over.

Everything now was as it had been before – though perhaps a little more ignoble, more ground in dust. As I walked through the town time past hung heavy on my feet. The face of a generation had disappeared completely. A few old women recognized me, throwing up their hands with an exclamation, then came running towards me with lowered voices as though we shared a secret. But of the men I had known there was little news, and such as there was, confused. Most of them, it seemed, were either dead or fled. The old women peered up at me with red-rimmed, clouded eyes, and each tale they told was different. My ex-boss, the hotel-keeper, who used to pray for Franco in his office, had been shot as a red spy ; he had died of pneumonia in prison ; he had escaped to France. Lalo, the hotel porter, had been killed on the barricades in Málaga; he ran a bar in Lyon; he was a barber in Jaén. Young Paco, the blond dynamiter of enemy tanks, was still a local fisherman – you could run into him at any time; no, he had blown himself up; he had married and gone to Majorca. Luiz, the carpenter, had betrayed his comrades and been stoned to death; he lived in Vélez Málaga; he sold chickens in Granada ...

In the end I gave up. There was no point in making any further inquiries. Nobody lied deliberately, but nobody wished to seem certain of the truth. For the truth, in itself, was unendurable.

I was restless and haunted in Castillo, and slept badly. Often I would go out before dawn and sit on the balcony, wrapped in a blanket, watching the dark sea's motions in the night. The slender strip of beach, gauzy with its nets, drew a sharp dividing frontier between the pure classic spaces of water and Castillo's earthy wretchedness. Time after time I sat thus, hunched up in my chair, watching new days grow slowly from the east. The moving patterns of these Mediterranean mornings seemed as formal as a sacred play. Each dawn brought the same sensations, the same dry whiff of ancient shores, the same slow Eastern look into the worlds of Egypt and the Phoenicians ...

At first there was nothing – a profound blue darkness running deep, laced by skeins of starlight and pale phosphorescent flashes. This four o'clock hour was a moment of utter silence, the indrawn breath of dark, the absolute, trance-like balance between night and day. Then, when it seemed that nothing would ever move or live or know the light again, a sudden hot wind would run over the invisible water. It was like a fore-blast of the turning world, an intimation that its rocks and seas and surfaces still stirred against the sun. One strained one's eyes, scarce breathing, searching for a sign. Presently it came. Far in the east at last the horizon hardened, an imperceptible line dividing sky and sea, sharp as a diamond cut on glass. A dark bubble of cloud revealed itself, warmed slowly, flushing from within like a seed growing, a kernel ripening, a clinker hot with a locked-in fire. Gradually the cloud throbbed red with light, then suddenly caught the still unrisen sun and burst like an expanding bomb. Flares and streamers began to fall into the sea, setting all things on fire. After the long unthinking darkness everything now began to happen at once. The stars snapped shut, the sky bled green, vermilion tides ran over the water, the hills around took on the colour of firebrick, and the great sun drew himself at last raw and dripping from the waves. Scarlet, purple and clinker-blue, the morning, smelling of thyme and goats, of charcoal, splintered rock and man's long sojourn around this lake, returned with a calling of dogs, the cough of asses and the hoarse speech of the fishermen going down to the working sea.

Some fishermen, of course, had been there all night, fishing far out with lamps; and now, in the overlapping light of dawn, they returned from the deep water to meet their poorer brothers setting out to fish the inshore shallows. In from the horizon, across the chill, flat, crimson silence, the little fleet came throbbing to the shore. As the vessels grounded, the fishermen of the night sprang red-legged into the water, wading ashore with cries and coughing, while a team of oxen, backing into the waves, hauled each boat up the sands.

Then the poor scratch fishermen of the morning took over, setting out in their long curved boats and rowing like madmen across the copper sea. The dark silhouettes of their craft, and of the bent men rowing, looked as old as Greece and revolved against the coloured water like ancient paintings on a pot. A man in the boat's high stern paid out a net, while the crew rowed lustily to his cries, kicking up little flames of spray. A net was laid in an arc off-shore, tethered to the land by its separate ends. Then two gangs of short, bandy-legged little men took these ends and began to haul it in again. It was a kind of slave labour, to be witnessed every morning. Panting, swearing, yelping and groaning, they toiled up the beach, while the heavy net, inch by inch, was laboriously hauled ashore.

After two hours of this mule-train labour the centre of the net, buoyed up by barrels, could be seen approaching the beach. Women and children began to appear in little groups on the sands, watching the net with intense black eyes. This was the peak moment of their day, moment of possible miracle though familiar disappointment, moment when the unknown catch of fish was drawn wallowing ashore. The women watched in silence, but excitement grew among the fishermen. The cries of the hauling men were louder, hoarser; their naked toes clawed deeper in the sand, they heaved, and threshed and tumbled, bending so low their beards almost scraped the ground. The boat crew ran up and down along the edge of the waves, barking like dogs and skipping in and out of the water. And all eyes were fixed on the patch of rippling foam where the long funnel of net rolled submerged with its catch.

At last, with a final burst, it was drawn ashore, a slack, black, serpentine shape twinkling with tiny scales. Seized and emptied upon the sand, before the watching eyes of the wives, the harvest was little enough – a pink mass of glutinous jellyfish and a few kilos of quivering sardines. The watchers and the exhausted fishermen drew in their breath, gazing silently at the wretched heap, and in it saw their poverty confirmed. For a while they stood in a ring, unspeaking, gazing down, while a Civil Guard, with cloak and rifle, drew near and shadowed all.

The disposal of the fish was a simple matter. Brown, scaly fingers sorted them into little heaps about the sand. Then the leader of the crew, in a croaking fatal voice, began to auction them on the spot. He mentioned a figure almost with shame. Two damp-faced dealers, bleary from their beds, approached and stood listlessly watching. 'Seventy-five,' said the fisherman, 'seventy-four ... seventy-three ...' As the price fell, so did his voice, as though he could not bear the women to hear such obscenities on his lips. At last, when his husky offer could sink no lower, one of the dealers nodded briefly, spat, and shovelled some loose change into the leader's hand. It was all over ; the pathetic price was shared, and the stunted men, still blown from their long labours, took their few pence in silence.

We watched four such auctions on four successive days and not once did the catch fetch more than thirty shillings. Half of this went to the owner of the boat and the rest was divided among some twenty men. By then there was scarcely enough left to buy bread with. On the worst mornings, when the price went down and down and there were no takers, the auctioneer would break off at last, click his teeth and stare at the mountains. This was the signal for the fishermen to share the catch among themselves. Then the sardines were counted out on the sands, scooped up into the aprons of the wives and borne away home. The children and the workless were left to scratch in the sand for the small fry which had passed unnoticed, and these they ate raw on the spot.

The morning's fishing, beginning at dawn, was usually over

by ten o'clock. From then on the men had nothing to do. So they spent their time lying face down on the sand, a row of jetsam above the shining sea, sleeping the ebb of their lives. The night fishermen caught bigger fish – rose-coloured salmonetti, species of mackerel, octopus and sometimes even tunny – but there was little profit in these either. A single dealer bought them for the Granada market and, lacking competition, he made his own prices.

It must be said that the men of Castillo were poor fishermen and even worse sailors. Their methods were antique, arduous and ineffective. They would only fish in the calmest waters. They often set out in a flurry of hysteria, swamped their boats, fouled their nets, fell overboard and were the most uncertain judges of weather. But the sterile waters were their worst enemy.

When the clamour of the morning's fishing was over, the town went quiet, and we sat on the balcony waiting for break- fast. No matter how long we waited we knew it wouldn't come till the hotel taps started whistling. Then Rosario, the chamber- maid, would appear jubilantly before us.

'They've turned the water on!' she'd cry. 'But a little pati- ence now and I will bring you your coffee.'

Half an hour later, a drumming of cloven hooves could be heard passing down the dusty street, and Rosario would appear again.

'The goats have come!' she'd announce rapturously. 'Now we have milk.'

And half an hour after that, proudly, as though each were a personal triumph of organization in the face of a long siege, the two sweet glasses of yellow coffee would be set before us. So it was every morning.

The days we spent here were spacious, slow and quiet. Still weak from my fever, I spent much of the daylight hours drink- ing white wine and watching the sea. Already, though it was

only January, the sun had marched northwards and strengthened, throwing each day upon the waves a trail of jagged stars
so dazzling they bruised the eyes. The warmth of the sun fell on
us like a treasure, and the daylight moved over the sea in great,
slow transpositions of colour, dying each night in purple dusks.
The cliffs and mountains soaked up the sunsets like red sponges
and the distant ragged edge of the Sierras shone blue as a blun-
ted saw.

After dark a boy would come and sing to us. The hotel-keeper
and his wife brought sardines and olives, the porter fetched
wine, Rosario pushed back the beds and she and Kati danced.
Later, the shutters were opened to admit the moon and we ended the night with story-telling. So passed the long casual days
of my convalescence; the sea with its patterns of boats and
men, the girls dancing in the dusk, the boy singing his tragic
songs along the path of the moon, and the haunted presence of
the town around us, smouldering in the dark.

Sitting one morning outside a sea-front café, eating cooked
liver and drinking the golden wine, we caught sight of a striking
figure advancing up the street towards us. He was a tall man,
wide hipped and narrow shouldered, shaped like a sherry cask,
and on the top of his large smooth head he wore a black beret
hardly bigger than a button. But what particularly drew one's
attention was not so much his size as his booming voice and
the extravagant, almost royal gestures with which he saluted
everyone in his path. To each of these, man, woman, child and
dog, he bellowed greetings as he came, and his face was lit by
a vast and insane smile. Loose-lipped and flabby-handed, rolling
and posturing on his tiny feet, he looked a terror.

'Watch him,' we said, as he approached. He caught our eye,
stopped dead, spun his great bulk on the points of his shoes,
swept off his hat, and bowed.

'Distinguished visitors!' he boomed. 'Welcome to Castillo.

Do you wish to pass a pleasant hour? Honour me then with your company, and I will show you my beautiful farm.'

Like ships becalmed, our slack sails stirred to his gusty voice; we rose, and to the winds of his pleasantries rode helplessly down the street before him.

'I am Don Paco,' he said. 'All the world knows me. They will tell you I have the best farm on the southern coast. I am loved by everyone and respected much. I am their father.'

We approached a group of washerwomen by the fountain. 'Ha! ladies,' he cried. They recoiled, broke up and ran scurrying into their houses. A dim old man came shuffling round the corner. Don Paco caught him by the shirt and pinned him against the wall.

'Well, uncle!' he bawled. 'Not dead yet? I never thought you'd get through the winter. It's a miracle.'

The old man wheezed and spluttered, wriggling in the other's grip.

'And how's that shameless daughter of yours?' Don Paco went on. 'Still breeding? Terrible she is. Thighs like serpents. Tell her from me she ought to be in the zoo.'

He hit the old man pleasantly in the stomach while the latter raised a thin defensive arm and cowered away.

'What a man you are with your dogs and daughters. Don't forget you owe me money – five duros it is now. Never mind, you can work it off. Come to the farm six o'clock tomorrow morning. Good idea. Good-bye.'

Don Paco released his grip and the old man crawled away, coughing and groaning as though he had been kicked by a horse. We left the town and Don Paco led us down a narrow lane shuttered on each side by tall green sugar-canes. The lane was waterlogged from a night of storm and we picked our way wetly along it.

'What a paradise!' cried Don Paco, skipping across a gigantic pothole. 'The most beautiful place in Europe and the best climate in the world.' He slipped on a pebble and went in up to his ankles in creamy mud. 'Have you not found it so?'

'Superb,' I said. 'Apart from the rain.'

'Nonsense,' he snapped. 'It never rains here. Mist and dew sometimes – but never rain.' He surveyed the flooded lane at his feet. 'This water comes from the Sierras – taste it' – he dipped a finger gingerly in the mud, licked it, gave a little shudder – 'pure snow, delicious, gift of heaven.' We went on. 'I tell you, Castillo wants for nothing. Sun, fruit, flowers all the year round. And so healthy. Have you ever felt better than you do at this moment?'

'Wonderful,' I said. 'Apart from a cold.'

'A *cold*!' snorted the man. 'Impossible. What you have is a slight nasal irritation due to the abundance of flowers in the place. No one has colds in Castillo. No one is ill.' He laughed. 'People live so long we have to shoot them. Out of kindness.'

We had come now to a walled garden, high, spiked and feudal. We paused before a wooden doorway. Don Paco kicked it open and it collapsed in a cloud of dust. Stepping over the ruin, Don Paco threw out his arms.

'Behold,' he said, 'my farm – el Rancho Grande.'

We saw an acre of land, square and well-watered, and set out with fruit trees and flowering broad beans. In a shed by the gateway a fat black pig lay perched on a pile of dung. Don Paco approached him with a loving cry. The pig grunted to his feet and ran squealing into a corner. Don Paco entered the sty, calling smooth endearments and making kissing noises with his lips.

'Look at him,' he crooned. 'Isn't he an angel?' He broke a loose piece off the feeding-trough and scratched the pig's back with it. The cornered pig made a scampering half-turn, snorting in terror. Don Paco glanced back at us over his shoulder, beaming with fatuous delight. 'Look how contented he is to see me,' he said. 'All day he cries for me. All day he waits for me to come. Ay, the lovely darling. Tomorrow I will kill him.'

We walked up a pathway lined with white roses. Violets and

tiny strawberries grew together on a bank. A fountain played under a soaring chestnut and birds sang loud in the branches. Don Paco gathered a bunch of the roses and gave them to me with a rolling bow.

'For your señora,' he said properly, and I passed them to Kati, who stood at his elbow. So we went round the tiny garden that was his farm, snug and green in a desert of rock. Strawberries, a withered custard apple, a handful of jasmine, all were showered on Kati, but always, of course, through me, with my permission. For Don Paco, farmer and booming bully, had a delicate sense of manners.

Next day a terrible thing happened. The night was hot and we played cards on the terrace above the moonlit milky water. The boy on the sand below us sang softly a list of griefs, and far out under the horizon a cluster of fishing-lamps burned red in the violet dark. The town was quiet, the cafés empty; even the radios had been turned off.

Suddenly we heard screams of laughter in the passage and plump Rosario come staggering in. She threw herself on the bed, tore off a boot and began to fan herself with it. For a while she sat shaking, unable to speak.

'Ay, what an occurrence,' she said at last, 'what an event more than anything.' She paused and wagged her head helplessly, exploding with giggles. 'My uncle it was. Pedro, the old one. He went out with the boats tonight as usual, but drunk as a mule. When they got three miles out they anchored, but poor Uncle Pedro, muddled in the head, he thought they'd just come home. So up he gets, says Good-night all, steps over the side, and hasn't been seen since.'

She went off, hooting, to tell the rest of the house. But poor Uncle Pedro, he'd come home all right. They found him, three days later, washed up in a neighbouring cove and already half-devoured by the fish. It was the biggest joke of the year in Castillo.

Our friend Don Paco, for all his pig-scratching and clownish antics, was one of the town's upper crust, owning much property and feared by all. There were several others of his breed in Castillo – Marco, the thin-lipped lecherous Mayor, who also ran the Casino; Díaz, the head of the fishing syndicate; and Villamarta, the sugar man, who owned the factory and the fields. These, with the Church, rode high and prosperously above the general poverty of the town. Theirs was the power and the glory, and they abused it in the usual, casual way, ignoring the fates of all past tyrannies and making their pile while the going was good. They seemed quite indifferent to what had gone before, what surely must come again. In one generation the Casino had three times been burnt to the ground by desperate fishermen, the sugar factory had twice been laid in ruins, the church had several times been well scorched by frenzied villagers. Yet Don Paco, Marco, Díaz, Villamarta and the Church still flourished. When revolt threatened, they knew what to do ; when the storm broke, they ran before it; they hid themselves till its violence was spent; and in the end they returned stronger than ever. The Casino and the sugar factory were restored. Villamarta raised a new villa, superbly vulgar, to dominate the town. And the Church, bearing its scorched images through the streets on holy days, saw the wretched incendiaries fall on their knees before them and weep for repentance.

We had come back to Castillo at a time of its periodic humiliation. The peasants of the field and the sea were beaten, and they lay low. Talking with them at night in the small bars inside the town, one saw their faces change at the mention of certain powers. Then their hoarse, African voices would sink to a whisper, they would shake their heads, put their fingers to their lips, clasp their hands together as though manacled, and go through the mime of a firing squad. The shadow of the Civil Guard, the long gun, the green satanic cloak, the black hat with its sombre wings – all these lay on them darkly. Meanwhile, they hacked at the sugar canes in the heat of the morning, or scratched for food among the rocks, or rowed out their lungs on the blood-red sea.

But in their salty, sunburnt eyes, in the twist of their copper lips, and in their silences, one saw what they could not say – a savage past, an inglorious present, a future choked with un-mentionable hopes.

6. Second View - Algeciras

The morning we left Castillo the sun was bright and pitiless, probing into the rags of the beggars and into the town's old wounds. The boatmen sprawled abandoned on the beach, the sea lay flat, clutching its miserable fish, the church and castle crumbled over all.

In our well-loaded bus we drove out westward, winding along the high coast road. And immediately the air cleared, shame and depression faded, and the deception of the light restored our spirits. It was a day of early spring, fragrant as water. Goat flocks browsed on the new-sprung herbs and blossoming almonds threw over the hills a veil of the lightest coral.

We were heading for Algeciras, along the Málaga road, and I was impatient to return to that blistering smuggler's town. It was along this same road, thyme-scented above the sea, that I had come walking an age ago before the wars, happy alone and in no hurry. Into these same olive groves, in a languor of lavender evenings, I climbed with my bread and wine to sleep rapturously among the rocks in a golden lust of exhaustion. It gave me a pain in the side to look at that landscape now.

We made a rapid journey along the coast, hundreds of feet above the dizzy sea. Boats with curved sails stood out on the blue water, Egyptian in outline, bird-like in shadow. The mountains to the north pursued us with purple peaks and clawed at the sea with great outcrops of rock across which we skipped on slender bridges. Then the wide bay of Málaga appeared with its sugar-coated villas and flowers and fermentations; and we paused here for a while, and drank the thick sweet wine.

Then on we went through stormier weather, by green and seething seas, plunging from sunshine to sunshine through marching walls of rain. At last, in the distant mists to seaward, like a ghost-ship far out on the horizon, a shaft of sunlight struck the slopes of Gibraltar and dressed it in golden fire. We raced through sparkling cork forests, through herds of black pigs, and over the sandy bed of the River Guadiaro. We climbed to a pass, saw Africa nose up out of the twilight, looked down at the dark currents snaking through the Straits, and passed under the Sierra de los Gazules. Then Algeciras was there, and we came down round the rusty roofs, bumped and blared through the cobbled streets, and pulled up finally on the familiar quayside.

We were back. After three months among the great white cities of Andalusia we had returned to our starting-point – this corrupt and raffish town which was to us the darling of them all. The evening harbour smelt sweetly of remembered shellfish, sherry and smuggled tobacco. Porters, touts, bootblacks and contrabandistas, addressing us by name, bore our bags and guitars into the 'Queen of the Sea'. A dozen girls from the attics descended upon Kati with cries and embraces. Ramón and Manolo advanced to wring my hand, eyes damped politely, compliments flew, and we were given our old room overlooking the bay. Thus we settled down to blow the rest of our money, and to wait for a passing ship to take us home.

In the mornings the bay was aflame. The sun leaned low on powerful haunches and licked the Sierras with its lion's tongue, leaving them red, rock-bare and raw. But Gibraltar, though leashed to the mainland by its strip of sand, seemed somehow to escape its livid breath, remaining cool and foreign, as though by protocol. I watched it from my balcony as I drank my breakfast. It lay on the waters like a glass-blue prawn, or crouched like a dog and threw off aircraft like fleas. Often it would spin from the cloudless Spanish skies a particular ball of mist which set it apart from the naked mainland and invested it daily with its own grey roof of English weather. Gun-metal faced, disciplined and dour, it could never do less than command our respect. But Algeciras, the foot-pad, beggarly poet thriving so seamily in its shadow, was, it must be said, invariably better company.

Kati returned to her friends in the attics, to that white-starched world of muted love songs, sibilant gossip and endless needle-work. Meanwhile I went back to the streets, to walk in the tang of the town and yield to those shiftless pleasures I never could resist.

I was shaved each morning by an old man whose shop faced the fishing-boats. His hands on the face were lighter than feathers, his brush moved over the skin as though in a cloud of warm air, and his razor left one glowing and renewed. He talked as he worked of the cities of the Incas, of Spain's old glories and the countlessness of the stars. And in the intervals between customers he took up the guitar and played it like a master.

Afterwards I went to the taverns and drank their golden sherries. In one, a group of men were discussing the baking of bread. They spoke with bright eyes, each echoing the other's wonder, as though describing a miracle. The best bread is like this, it comes from the wheat of Mora, it is shaped thus, marked thus, placed in the oven so. The fire must be spread wide, sprinkled with charcoal, glowing like the crust of the sun. The baked bread opens thus, turns cream and gold like a ripe chrysanthe-mum, is crisp yet tender to the teeth, and tastes like manna. The best bread is from Portonegro, the old man Charro bakes it, his loaves are like girls' breasts, all milk and sunshine. To eat such bread one wants neither fruit nor meat. No, it is a meal in itself. And so it went. Such rapt remembering of skill and flavour, such poetry of gesture, scooping, rolling, shaping the loaves. Here was speech and movement not yet enslaved by either jargon or the machine ; phrases out of Homer and the Bible, by men who had read neither.

In another tavern a slender whore stood weeping and drinking by the bar. Her face was white and scarred round the eyes and mouth, and she wore a halo of tangled hair. Her smooth red dress clung tightly to her body as though she had been dipped in wax. 'I dreamed last night of my dead father,' she was saying. 'He was beautiful. Like a lovely horse. The only man I ever loved. He is dead. There are no men left in the world.' She hung over the bar and wept into her wine, with eyes for no one, speaking to herself.

Out in the street the market buzzed and murmured, slashed here and there by the sharp cries of a fish-seller. I wandered here and saw a madman, hooded in a cloak, run through the crowd. Every so often he would pause and uncover his cropped head and raise his ravaged face to the sky and howl and stick pins in his throat. Women went up to him and thrust bread in his pockets. The boys and children laughed.

Also in the market-place there was a ballad singer, chanting some recent crime from Alicante. It was a dull crime on the whole, about a schoolboy, beautiful and good, whose mother gave him a peseta each morning to buy a cake. He saved up the money instead and bought a lottery ticket. He won, and in his excitement told his schoolmaster, who murdered him to get the prize. Thirty-seven verses, to a rigid air, told us the tale, demanding our pity and horror. A listening crowd drank up the awful song, nodding among themselves when the last verse pointed out how many evil deeds were committed for money. A printed sheet of the words could be bought for a penny.

Near the Post Office a boy came up to me with a bird in his hands, a yellow-crested bird with slack wings and rolling, unconscious eyes. 'It is a jay,' said a bootblack, watching. The boy held it up for me to see but its head hung down limply. 'Is it dying?' I asked. 'No,' said the boy, 'it is always like that – a sad bird.' And he buttoned it up in his shirt, leaving the dull head bobbing out like a sick old man in bed.

Up in the Plaza Alta I met Manolo, who was walking hands clasped with a blond young man. 'I want you to meet Isidro,' said Manolo. 'He is my special friend. We have been walking in the park discussing philosophy – but things very deep.' Isidro shook my hand and smiled, as though I would hardly believe how deep those things were. He had a long sensitive face, a limping foot, and was a baker by profession. We sat down at a café table under a shrivelled orange tree and Manolo wrote down for me a selection of the afternoon's philosophical findings. These told me that the world was round, that God was love, that night must fall, five beans make a poor meal, and death comes to all men in the end. After that, we took a bottle of wine and faced each other, flexing our wits for the task before us. Then each in turn wrote an epigram on the table-top, and the best in each round was recorded in a book. By the coming of dusk we had squared many a circle and dazzled ourselves with our brains. What low whistles and shaking of heads there were at our brilliance. It was as good as dominoes or dice.

A tubby little American had arrived at the hotel, on leave from Africa, where he had been building air-bases. He had small blue eyes, a chubby face, a simple drawl, and his name was Ben. He seemed lone and lost and not at all sure why he had come to Spain in the first place, except that he had wanted to get out of Africa. Africa terrified him. That night we ate together, and he gazed at us with popping eyes, breathless and sweating, as though amazed to find himself still alive.

'Ah just don't fancy that Africa at all,' he said. 'No sah. Them folks had me real scared.' He puffed out his lips and looked over his shoulder. 'Ah can't understand it. Them Frenchies seem to hate us Americans. Charge us six times over for a drink and then insult us cause we don't know the lingo. As fer them Arabs!' His eyes went round and wide. 'Why, they'll kill you fer two dollars.'

After dinner we sat round on the terrace drinking coffee and coñac.

'Does me good talkin' to you folks,' he said. 'Keeps me out of trouble. Not that I aim to do much drinkin' anyhow. Ah'm right off it, you unnerstand.'

He was forty-nine, and a grandfather, he said; married when he was fourteen to a girl of twenty-three. She was home in California, but when he spoke of her she seemed to sit at his trembling elbow.

'Nevah drink back home,' he said. 'Mah wife won't let me. Not since that time in San Diego. Got drunk there one night. Boy, it was terrible. Ah was drivin' home an' got picked up by a patrol man. He said he was goin' to take me in – so ah hit 'im!' He clenched his fist and hit out, then dropped his eyes and giggled, afraid of himself.

'Liquor makes me wild,' he said shyly. 'Ah'm part Cherokee, ya see. Look at mah cheek-bones.'

In the fume of the red-lit café he raised his head, and we looked, and sure enough he *was* Cherokee, his cheek-bones naked in the night, his small eyes bright and mad.

'Ah thought that patrol man was doin' me an injustice,' he went on, 'so ah knocked him down. He fell on the curb there an' it peeled his head right back. Ah was in real trouble then, believe me. But ah got me a crooked lawyer an' a crooked judge an' they charged me a thousand dollars an' told me to get out of town. Boy, ah was lucky. Ah could have done time for what I did that night.'

We were going to a cabaret and asked him to come with us. But he excused himself, trembling slightly. He said he'd have another coñac and go to bed. We left him there looking small and lost, chastened by memory.

The next morning there was a great stir among the chambermaids. They came giggling to our room to tell us that the American was lying in bed covered with lipstick, groaning, moaning, and ringing bells, and that nobody could understand what he said.

I went to his room to see what I could do. The round, childish face lay on the pillow, pink and ashamed, and a trembling hand tried to cover his red-smeared mouth.

'Am ah glad to see you,' he shuddered. 'Ah'm in real trouble.

Just walked out fer a little drink last night an' got mah wallet stolen. Had all mah money in it – tickets, passport an' everything. God damn it, they even poisoned mah liquor!' He held his head in his hands. 'What am ah goin' to do now?'

I went downstairs to make some enquiries, and they told me what had happened. When the bar closed last night, Ben had persuaded the barman to take him to a dance hall. There he had danced with the girls, treated everybody, got very drunk and disappeared. Later some fishermen had found him in a brothel where he was causing quite a sensation. He had nailed his wallet to the wall and was saying that the girl who could kick that high could have it. After that he'd passed out, and the fishermen had taken charge of both Ben and his wallet and carried him home. The wallet they'd left in his boots.

And sure enough there it was. Ben took it from me with shaking hands and fumbled feverishly, but clumsily, through its contents. Everything was intact, including 500 dollars cash. He almost sobbed with relief; then pulled himself together and thought he'd like some breakfast – not much, just ham and eggs and cawfee.

Kati went off to the kitchen to arrange this for him, and we didn't see him again till noon. The Seville bus was due to leave, and the porter had loaded the American's bags on it, when suddenly we saw him coming briskly down the street carrying a great armful of irises and daises.

'Ah brought these few blooms for your lady, sah,' he said, and handed them to her with solemn dignity. He was shaved and spruce now, a southern gentleman. 'It was a pleasure to meet you mam, an' you sah. You've been real kind to me. If evah you're in California . . .'

He took off his snap-brimmed hat, exposed his rosy pate to the sun, bowed, then mounted the bus. With a drunken lurch it bore him away, carrying him to his doom.

Isidro, the baker-philosopher, had now met Kati and fallen in love with her. Each day he hobbled up the street to bring us gifts of new-baked bread. When we met at the cafés in the evening to write our epigrams he was dignified and sad, his manners always perfect, though his written thoughts veered from abstract considerations of the cosmos to those of romantic though melancholy speculation. Manolo, the waiter, treated him as a sick man and was tender, like a nurse. But night and day Isidro haunted the quayside in front of the hotel, walking slowly up and down and trailing his limp leg after him. Our room began to burst with bread, and smuggling it out to the beggars became a major conspiracy. Mysterious serenaders appeared under our window, hired by the baker, who hovered ghost-like in a doorway while they played. The daily gift of loaves grew more and more exotic in shape, their crusts decorated with hearts and flowers, with moons and stars, with pretty angels, even with our names – though these never appeared together on the same loaf.

Then, early one morning, Isidro appeared at the door in his best suit, tense and smiling, with a jar of wine in his hand. It was his saint's day, he said, and his father had given him a holiday. So he had arranged a picnic in the cork-woods and he invited us to come. Manolo, of course, was with him, standing a little aside like a keeper, and with his great dog's eyes he signalled that we must accept.

But we were glad to go. It was a hot and hazy day, and Isidro promised us trees and water. So we bought some fruit, and a bottle of coñac, and took a conveyance into the hills. It was a different country there from the dusty coast ; a wooded valley, green and fresh, with grass and flowers among rocks and a mountain stream running cool. The valley was narrow, almost a gorge, and birds flashed through the cork trees like motes before the eye. The shining stream slipped smoothly, silently, over the tumbled boulders ; brown and white goats passed by with swinging bells, and high overhead, in the blue lane of the sky, dark eagles circled slowly.

We sat ourselves down on sun-warm rocks and passed the

wine-cask round. Warmth and idleness ran languorously through our bodies. Isidro unwrapped cheese and meat and a huge loaf which he had baked the night before, and all our names were worked across the crust, entwined in leaves and lilies. So we ate, and drank, and stretched out under the trees, and floated the wine in the stream to keep it cool. Meanwhile Manolo, rather drunk, sang sad songs of the Asturias, which was his home, and Isidro, in the intervals, gazed into the water and explained portentously the symbolism of it.

From the forested heights of these mountains, they told us, one could see the whole of the Straits; the ships passing, the leaping dolphins and the tides sliding in from the Atlantic like long blue snakes. One could see westward into the Gulf of Cádiz and far south into the mint-green hills of Morocco.

'In Morocco,' said Isidro, gazing mournfully at Kati, 'the women cover their faces, and all wives are kept hidden.'

'A good thing,' said Manolo primly.

They told us of the life in the higher valleys here, and of the robbers who inhabited them. Kidnapping was their special line, and they were particularly fond of merchants and bankers, whom they carried off and held for ransom, hiding them in cunning discomfort till the money was paid.

'Love is a bandit,' said Isidro heavily.

'And the heart its ransom,' added Manolo mechanically.

They told us of the hermits who lived here in caves, old bearded men who spent their days in prayer, living on nuts and berries. They were holy men, fleeing the temptations of the flesh.

'I would be a hermit,' said Isidro.

'It is a life of torment,' said Manolo.

'But less cruel than the world,' said Isidro, gazing again at Kati.

So we passed the afternoon, finishing the wine slowly to a pleasant mixture of high thoughts and romantic melancholy. Then at last, in a blue dusk, we left the valley and walked back to the town. A curved moon, like a quartered orange, hung low over Morocco, and the wide sky filled with big bright stars. We discussed them, and the cosmic spaces between, to which sexless abstractions Isidro's mind seemed happily to have returned. We passed under the great arches of the Viaduct and entered the town in the chill of the night wind, and the lights of Gibraltar filled the bay like a spiral nebulae.

There are bars in Algeciras where a glass of wine and a plate of shrimps cost only twopence; where it takes an hour to spend a shilling; where a bootblack has only to see you to press drinks upon you; and where processions of strangers are for ever offering you glasses of coñac with proud gestures of courtly friendship. Any attempt to return the favour is discouraged by a shocked shaking of the head. You are a traveller, they say; it is our privilege to make you welcome. In the face of such formal hospitality there is nothing to be done but to drink and talk of bulls, answer questions about one's country, and discuss politics by vague allusions.

It was in one such bar that I met Ricardo, of Bilboa. He was a lean, military-looking young man, with a thin black moustache and a sharp blue suit. He was a commercial traveller, and his clean, classical Spanish cut through the husky Andalusian dialect like a sword. But he was a nervous man, always looking over his shoulder, constantly moving me away from suspicious persons, his bright eyes never still. As we drank and talked he summed me up, seemed to find me safe, and slowly revealed himself. As a captain in the Republican Army he had fought against Franco. He had been captured at last and sentenced to death. By some casual mistake of book-keeping the sentence was never carried out; he was abandoned in jail and forgotten. For many days he lay alone in the darkness of a small underground cell in some fortress near Teruel. He lived by chewing straw and licking the water from the walls. At last, with a metal cup, he made a tunnel and escaped. He found friends who clothed him, the war ended, he took a new name and got a job. From then on he has travelled like a ghost around the south of Spain, unable to return to his family.

I thought it mad of him to tell me all this, but he seemed eager to talk. We moved restlessly from bar to bar. He could not keep still, and kept pointing out to me people he knew (or suspected) to be secret police or informers. And all the time he talked, while his eyes went dark and wet, his body shook and his voice broke with despair.

Ricardo was an educated man, slender in thought and body, sincere, sentimental in the best sense, and a believer once in heaven and hell. He still could not understand what went wrong. The aspirations of his comrades in arms had seemed so honest and simple. How, he asked, could these hopes have been termed criminal, how could they have been condemned and abandoned by the world, to be met only by bombs and bullets, imprisonment and massacre? He talked of the miners of Asturias, their naïve ambitions, their bewilderment when the world named them mobsters, bandits, outlaws. Their friends from abroad sent them nothing but poems, greetings and votes of solidarity. The rest came with fire and explosives. So they fought the tanks with bare hands and bottles, threw rocks at the machine-guns, and shot at the dive-bombers with ancient muskets. It was then that they realized the futility of good intentions. For they were defeated. They were bound, fettered, stripped and starved. They were herded into bull-rings, lined up against the walls of churches, and shot as though diseased. And when the first paroxysms of their conquerors had passed, having slaughtered a million or so of these amazed but simple men, the rest were imprisoned and left, crowded like rats in holes in the ground, till they fought each other for what food there was and saw even their comradeship degraded.

It was fifteen years now since the end of that civil war, yet the prisons were still full, while young wives grew old slaving for bread to feed their ageing men.

'All we wished for,' said Ricardo, 'was an honest life. A life

of clean breath and happy conscience. We wished to raise ourselves a few steps from the dust only. Why were those in the
high chairs so terrified? We in Spain were the first victims of
that fear. Hired gunmen were sent against us, and they slaughtered the best of us. Why did none of you stop this thing? It
was the beginning of evil. All the world is a prison now. And the
spirit of man is polluted.'

Ricardo, in his bright suit, his pockets stuffed with pamphlets
praising his firm's sardines, was the living shame of his age,
hiding from the secret police and from his conscience. He could
not forgive himself for having been spared, but it was too late to
be a martyr now.

Meanwhile the police moved here and there; the hoarse fishermen in the taverns lowered their voices and made tormented
jokes about the Powers; and the generals drove to Mass in their
big black cars and back through saluting streets.

It was early March and spring had come. The skies were full
of the swoop and squeak of swallows. Geraniums flowered on
all the houses, and in the fields the beans were up and the wheat
was a bright high green. In the heat of the day we walked to the
beach which lay two miles out of the town. A green dust of
herbs lay over the hills and small flowers grew on the cliffs.
Through long hot days we lay on the beach, sleeping and bath-
ing at intervals, while large white cows walked the sands before
us and an old crone gathered seaweed.

Above the sea the strong sun climbed the sky, and the coastal
cities of Morocco shone white as apparitions, like flickering
crystals, like cameos set in glass. There was no wind, and the
small tide came in like a sigh, stealing imperceptibly across the
weed-green stones. I dozed easily in the wine-scented heat, and
woke to see Kati standing in the still water like a carved Greek
statue cut off at the thigh. Along the soft blue edge of the horizon ships moved like cut-out toys – tankers tramps and battle-
ships, and liners heading for home.

They were gentle days; days torn from this March summer which would mean an extra summer in our lives. On the cliffs there were goats and horses nibbling the new-sprung green, and the sonorous chime of the goat-bells was like a musical skin over the landscape.

Our way back to the town lay through fields of wheat, and here, upon eminences overlooking the sea, we found elaborate concrete gun-sites, set to command the Straits, newly built but already decaying. Lizards inhabited them only, and flowers grew over the gun-slits. Inside, on the wall of one, was written: 'Here I loved Manuela.'

Entering the town we visited the families who lived in the ruins of the unfinished Casino. A network of girders stood at the sea's edge, and these, with the aid of tarpaulins, the families had made into homes. It was an active, noisy little suburb, running with pigs and children. The children had named me 'Man of Iron' because they once found me sleeping among thistles. When I pass by now they punch me and say 'Dong!' then hop and skip, pretending they've hurt their hands. The women take in washing, which they hang on the girders to dry. The men sit idly, watching their children run, amazed at the fecundity of their loins, the sterility of their life.

A company of singers and dancers had come to the theatre by the bull-ring. They were heading for North Africa, but paused here for a night to earn their passage money. The troupe was led by Caracol and his lustrous daughter Luisa Ortega, and although the show was not due to begin till midnight we drank black coffee and went to see it.

The theatre was uncomfortable and shabby – rows of hard chairs, a urine-scented bar, a floor littered with unswept popcorn shells, and a bare-board stage curtained with orange paper. But nobody cared much about the setting; a show of this nature enjoyed an immediate acceptance by the audience and the company itself was well aware of this and showed a superb confidence in consequence.

After the usual delays the lights went down to an empty stage, and to a nervous whispering of guitars, unseen and fluent, warming up in the wings with the murmur of tropical insects. Such tentative exploration of phrasing and technique was the formal prelude on such occasions, building up atmosphere and tightening our expectant nerves. At last the rhythms strengthened, striking imperative chords, calling the dancers forth, till one by one they entered, erect and vibrant, each different yet perfect, moving with a stylized nobility and grace that was rigid with tradition and devotion to the dance. They were all young girls, and their dark hair, threaded with flowers, was greased and watered in shining curls. They all wore crucifixes, and their flounced dresses were fantastic – all white, or red, or black – and they moved across the darkened stage like figures of fire and ice, trembling, flickering, weaving and stamping, upright as flame and supple as smoke, blown hot and cold by the throbbing breath of the guitars. The girls' faces were all alike, masks of Araby, heavily painted, but each possessing a formal perfection that was real, based on the Moorish brow and cheek-bone, the tormented mouth, the huge and slanting eyes. And the severe setting of their hair, coiled like tar around the flowers, broke loose always in the frenzy of the dance and fell in wet curls over the naked shoulders.

These dancers, who were they? – nameless girls of Seville and Ronda, no better than most, but moving with the enthralled precision of priestesses, lost in the magic of every step. Here were none of the glazed smiles and loose kicking of the legs that passes for dancing on northern stages. For in Spain all girls danced, and most danced well, but you did not dance in public unless your dancing reached this trance-like passion and control. The level of popular criticism was too high to suffer anything but the best.

After the girls came the star, Luisa Ortega, with her dark, beautiful Indian face and anguished, mobile mouth, to sing a series of songs she had written herself – songs of love, pain, the Virgin and 'mi Granada'. Her glittering eyes were like black fruits, juicy with tears, and in the negroid curls of her hair white roses hung like sheep's wool caught on thorns. The words of her songs, perhaps, were not distinguished, but her passion clothed them in such fires that they spread like pentecostal flames over the audience and reduced the men to throaty, gasping cheers. Her voice was curious; hard metallic, yet fluent as the iron-work of Seville. But at the climax of each song an explosive heat of sentiment seemed to fuse it into a wild orgasm of phrasing, so that she fled each time from the stage to a storm of compassionate cries.

The rest of the night was devoted to that most fundamental, most mysterious of all encounters in Andalusian folk-music – the cante flamenco. Three people only take part and the stage itself is reduced to bareness. First comes the guitarist, a neutral, dark-suited figure, carrying his instrument in one hand and a kitchen chair in another. He places the chair in the shadows, sits himself comfortably, leans his cheek close to the guitar and spreads his white fingers over the strings. He strikes a few chords in the darkness, speculatively, warming his hands and his imagination together. Presently the music becomes more confident and free, the crisp strokes of the rhythms more challenging. At that moment the singer walks into the light, stands with closed eyes, and begins to moan in the back of his throat as though testing the muscles of his voice. The audience goes deathly quiet, for what is coming has never been heard before, and will never be heard again. Suddenly the singer takes a gasp of breath, throws back his head and hits a high barbaric note, a naked wail of sand and desert, serpentine, prehensile. Shuddering then, with contorted and screwed-up face, he moves into the first verse of his song. It is a lament of passion, an animal cry, thrown out, as it were, over burning rocks, a call half-lost in air, but imperative and terrible. At first, in this wilderness, he remains alone, writhing in the toils of his words, whipped to more frenzied utterance by the invisible lash of the guitar.

At last, the awful solitude of his cry is answered by a dry shiver of castanets off-stage, the rustle of an awakened cicada, stirred by the man's hot voice. Gradually the pulse grows more staccato, stronger, louder, nearer. Then slow as a creeping fire, her huge eyes smoking, her red dress trailing like flames behind her, the girl appears from the wings. Her white arms are raised like snakes above her, her head is thrown back, her breasts and belly taut, while from her snapping, flickering fingers the black mouths of the castanets hiss and rattle, a tropic tongue, eloquent and savage. The man remains motionless, his arms outstretched, throwing forth loops of song around her and drawing her close towards him. And slowly, on drumming feet, she advances, tossing her head and uttering little cries. Once caught within his orbit she begins to circle him, weaving and writhing, stamping and turning; her castanets chatter, tremble, whisper; her limbs are entangled in his song, coiled in it, reflecting each parched and tortured phrase by the voluptuous postures of her body. And so they act out together long tales of love: singing, dancing, joined but never touching.

This form of the flamenco, the most dramatic and exhausting, has fused both song and dance into an erotic perfection such as I believe exists nowhere else in the world. Only the moral embargoes of Spanish society, coupled with its natural paganism, could produce such a volcanic yet exquisitely controlled sexuality as this. The man is all voice; the woman all pride and hunger. While his song climbs into ecstasies of improvisation she coils in toils and sobs and throbs around him. And always there is the invisible guitar, whipping them delicately from the dark, feeding their secret fevers.

Now comes our last days – with the boat that was to carry us home already signalled from the Suez. The March sun grew to summer heat and the girls put on their thinnest, most liquid

dresses. On the white walls of taverns, and under the arches of
bridges, bright posters appeared to announce the spring fiestas.
It was a bad time to leave, and we felt like children condemned
to their cold beds just when the downstairs party was due to
begin. But there was nothing for it; our money was spent, our
tickets bought ; and Tuesday, with the homeward boat, moved
steadily nearer Gibraltar.

How crystal sharp the town appeared suddenly under its arc
of mountains, how bright the flowers and washing on the roofs,
how profound the shadows thrown on the cobbled streets. Each
simple gesture of beggar and fisherman assumed an almost
mythological significance, each pedlar's cry seemed invested
with timeless poetry. 'I have caramels, tomatoes and ham from
the hills!' 'I have octopus from the sea, most rich and good!'
'I have a few numbers the best and most fortunate!' 'Limpia!
Limpia!' 'Africa de hoy!'

The ferry came in with its crooks and tourists; the smugglers
snuffled in doorways their pockets bulging; the green-cloaked
policemen leant dozing on their muskets; and each night the
fishing-boats put out over the flat sea to hunt for tunny and
cigarettes.

In the town the housewives went daily to the church, to pray
for a cheap piece of fish, or strength for their husbands' thighs.
The girls in groups walked through the streets parading their
unassailable bodies. The boys sat daylong at café tables discussing football and philosophy. And the beggar children, sore-
lipped and with eyes diseased, scampered in gutters, smiling
their beautiful smiles.

Perched in this southern town, one's thoughts already moving
towards home, one felt intensely the great square weight of
Spain stretching away north behind one; felt all there was to
leave, from these palm-fringed tropic shores to the misty hills
of Bilboa; the plains of la Mancha, Sierras of pine and snow, the
golden villages perched on their gorges, wine smells of noon
and sweet wood smoke of evening, the strings of mules crawl-

ing through huge brown landscapes, the rarity of grass, the
wood ploughs scratching the dusty fields, and the families at
evening sitting down to their plates of beans. One heard the
silences of the Sierras, the cracking of sun-burnt rocks, the sharp
jungle voices of the women, the tavern-murmur of the men,
the love songs of the girls rising at dawn, the sobbing of asses
and whine of hungry dogs. Spain of cathedrals, palaces, caves
and hovels; of blood-stained bull-rings and prison-yards; of
weeping Virgins, tortured Christs, acid humour and incomparable song – all this lay anchored between the great troughs of
its mountains, locked in its local dialects, bound by its own sad
pride.

Spain is but Spain, and belongs nowhere but where it is. It is
neither Catholic nor European but a structure of its own, forged
from an African-Iberian past which exists in its own austere
reality and rejects all short-cuts to a smoother life. Let the dollars come, the atom-bomb air-bases blast their way through the
white-walled towns, the people, I feel, will remain unawed,
their lips unstained by chemical juices, their girls unslacked,
and their music unswung. For they possess a natural resistance
to civilization's more superficial seductions, based partly on the
power of their own poetry, and partly on their incorruptible
sense of humour and dignity.

The home-bound liner lay anchored across the bay, and Juan,
one of the waiters, brought us the news. Juan, in summer, was
a bull-fighter, and was always showing his scars. 'I have brought
a beautiful picture of myself being tossed by a bull,' he said. 'It
is in colour. Keep it to remember me by.' As we packed our
bags came others with gifts of farewell. Ramón gave us a drawing of his child and some wine from his wife's vineyard; Manolo, a sheaf of poems; Isidro, a loaf flavoured with saffron and
currants. Friends from the taverns showered me with sherry
and bottle-openers, and an old fisherman handed me some cop-
las which he had composed to Kati's beauty.

The last morning was a grape-blue mist of still air and water.

Manolo and Isidro, solemn-faced, dressed in their best, were to take us to the harbour. The chambermaids descended upon Kati with tears and kisses, begging her to return, and giving her gifts of lace. Then we gathered all our luggage, guitars, tambourines and jars of wine, piled them on a hand-cart and set off for the tender. Girls on the quays were packing fish in ice and palm leaves. The oily water of the harbour floated with lottery tickets and orange peel, the debris of a discarded winter. The peaks of the mountains towards Málaga appeared out of the blue mist like a froth of burnt sugar.

The tender blew its siren and we climbed the gangway on to its throbbing deck. Manolo and Isidro stood looking up at us from the dockside, their hats in their hands, their eyes like dark olives.

'This is your home,' said Manolo formally. 'And my house is yours.'

Isidro said nothing. The siren blew again.

'Go with God,' said Manolo, looking at me.

'And return a widow,' muttered Isidro, looking at Kati.

Then we drew away from the harbour and from the town, and headed across the smooth waters of the bay, to the waiting ship, to the smell of brewed tea, to the shuffle of bridge-cards and the snows of London. And Spain slid back from our eyes into the mist, leaving us lost and footless on a naked sea.

More about Penguins

Penguinews, which appears every month, contains details of all the new books issued by Penguins as they are published. From time to time it is supplemented by *Penguins in Print*, which is a complete list of all books published by Penguins which are in print. (There are well over three thousand of these.)

A specimen copy of *Penguinews* will be sent to you free on request, and you can become a subscriber for the price of the postage. For a year's issues (including the complete lists) please send 30p if you live in the United Kingdom, or 60p if you live elsewhere. Just write to Dept EP, Penguin Books Ltd, Harmondsworth, Middlesex, enclosing a cheque or postal order, and your name will be added to the mailing list.

Some other books published by Penguins are described on the following pages.

Note : *Penguinews* and *Penguins in Print* are not available in the U.S.A. or Canada

J. R. Ackerley

My Father and Myself

J. R. Ackerley was born into a seemingly conventional bourgeois
family living in Richmond. His mother, a frail ex-actress; his
father, a well-to-do, heavily-moustached Edwardian paterfamilias.
   Only after his father's death did the author discover that 'Dad'
had long maintained a mistress and three daughters in Barnes ...
   In unravelling the facts behind his father's duplicity – which
include an odd relationship as a trooper with a mysterious Count
de Gallatin and eccentric entry into the banana business –
Ackerley also reveals much of himself: from schoolboy to
frontline subaltern; from shiftless student to tireless searcher
for the Ideal Friend in the twilight of homosexual London.

We Think the World of You

The love between friends, Johnny, young and feckless, and
Frank, middle-aged and devoted – and their love for Johnny's
beautiful pedigree bitch, Evie: these are the main themes of
this extraordinary novel. And peripheral to these themes: the
jealousy and the break-down of friendship in the context of
Johnny's prison sentence and Frank's platonic relationship with
his mother; the hatred of Johnny's stepfather for Frank; the
consuming jealousy of Johnny's slatternly young wife; and
throughout, the beautiful dog becomes more and more the
creature around which their relationships revolve ...
'A miniature masterpiece that will become a classic' –
Raymond Mortimer
'What a brilliant book this is!' – *New Statesman*

Not for sale in the U.S.A.

Elizabeth Jane Howard

Something in Disguise

In this compulsive, entertaining novel, Elizabeth Jane Howard
sets out to explore the personal and social interactions of a
contemporary family with a charming candour.

Alice – innocent, painfully shy and very lonely, who marries
a man much older than herself to escape a home that is
becoming a prison.

Oliver – handsome, intelligent, drifting through an endless
series of careers and girls in a restless search for involvement.

Elizabeth – who discovers that love, for her, leads to unhappiness.

May, their mother, whose second marriage to Colonel Herbert
Browne-Lacey turns out to be a terrible mistake, making her
life a struggle to keep the peace between her children and her
boring, self-important husband.

Herbert – her husband, who keeps secret liaisons with a woman
in London, has a past that is suspect, and future plans for May
that are highly dangerous.

Not for sale in the U.S.A.

E. F. Benson

Mapp and Lucia

Mapp, a formidable spinster, has long reigned as social queen of Tilling, a picture-book seaside town. Then Lucia comes to Tilling ... and it's total war!

E. F. Benson gives us a round-by-round commentary on Mapp and Lucia's desperate struggle for power. Rebuff and reprisal; spying and prying; honeyed exchange fraught with dark menace ...

This book has all the qualities of vintage gossip. More, it catches and holds with deadly accuracy the extinct world of pre-war rentier society; the majors, padres and lady water-colourists – with their private incomes and servant problems, their bridge teas and games of golf.

Lucia's Progress

Lucia, sweet smiling mistress of Machiavellian intrigue; Mapp, champion of oblique innuendo and the deadly thrust ... who will be queen of Tilling?

Round after round, Lucia plays darting David to Mapp's floundering Goliath. Lucia cleans up on the Stock Market and Mapp, now married to her Major 'Benjy' believes herself to be pregnant; Lucia buys Mapp's house and, during conversions thinks she's struck a rich seam in Roman remains ... and all Tilling stares in wide-eyed, slack-jawed amazement as the rivals explode each other's pretensions.

Continuing his brilliantly-observed celebration of pre-war leisured life E. F. Benson's merry widows with their 'treasured' maids; his ageing water-colourists with their private incomes, their golf and their bridge may have passed on in fact ... but Lucia's Progress assures them golden immortality.

Not for sale in the U.S.A. or Canada

Laurie Lee

Cider with Rosie

Cider with Rosie puts on record the England we have traded
for the petrol engine. Recalling life in a remote Cotswold village
nearly forty years ago, Laurie Lee conveys the semi-peasant
spirit of a thousand-years-old tradition.

'This poet, whose prose is quick and bright as a snake ... a
gay, impatient, jaunty and in parts slightly mocking book; a
prose poem that flashes and winks like a prism' – H. E. Bates in
the *Sunday Times*

As I Walked Out One Midsummer
Morning

It was 1935. The young man walked to London from the security
of the Cotswolds to make his fortune. He was to live by playing
the violin and by a year's labouring on a London building site.
Then, knowing one Spanish phrase, he decided to see Spain. For
a year he tramped through a country in which the signs of
impending civil war were clearly visible.

Thirty years later Laurie Lee has captured the atmosphere of the
Spain he saw with all the freshness and beauty of a young man's
vision, creating a lyrical and lucid picture of the beautiful and
violent country that was to inextricably involve him.

'A marvellous book' – Kenneth Allsop, BBC, *The World of
Books*

'A beautiful piece of writing' – John Raymond in the *Observer*

Not for sale in the U.S.A.